Series / Number 01-064

Decision-Making
in Smaller Democracies:
The Consociational "Burden"

JEFFREY OBLER
JÜRG STEINER
University of North Carolina at Chapel Hill

GUIDO DIERICKX
University of Antwerpen

 SAGE PUBLICATIONS / Beverly Hills / London

For information address:

SAGE PUBLICATIONS, INC.
275 South Beverly Drive
Beverly Hills, California 90212

SAGE PUBLICATIONS LTD
St George's House / 44 Hatton Garden
London EC1N 8ER

International Standard Book Number 0-8039-0759-1

Library of Congress Catalog Card No. L.C. 77-72062

FIRST PRINTING

When citing a professional paper, please use the proper form. Remember to cite the
correct Sage Professional Paper series title and include the paper number. One of the
two following formats can be adapted (depending on the style manual used):

(1) NAMENWIRTH, J. Z. and LASSWELL, H. D. (1970) "The Changing Language of
American Values." Sage Professional Papers in Comparative Politics, 1, 01-001.
Beverly Hills and London: Sage Pubns.

OR

(2) Namenwirth, J. Zvi and Lasswell, Harold D. 1970. *The Changing Language of
American Values.* Sage Professional Papers in Comparative Politics, vol. 1, series no.
01-001. Beverly Hills and London: Sage Publications.

CONTENTS

Decision-Making
in Smaller Democracies:
The Consociational "Burden"

JEFFREY OBLER
JÜRG STEINER
University of North Carolina at Chapel Hill
GUIDO DIERICKX
University of Antwerpen

1. INTRODUCTION

A major item in the daily news is the outbreak of violence among cultural groups in various countries. Examples that come easily to mind are Northern Ireland, Lebanon, Cyprus, and South Africa. In our view, it is an important task for comparative politics to explain the outbreak of such violence and to propose means for more peaceful relations. Several political scientists have addressed this problem by developing the theory of consociationalism. It was first presented in a systematic way at the 1967 World Congress of the International Political Science Association in Brussels by Lijphart (1967) and Lehmbruch (1967a). Working independently, they came to similar conclusions. They set out to explain the level of violence among strongly developed cultural groups. The crux of the theory is that the decision-making behavior of the political elites affects the level of violence among cultural groups. This was a new theoretical development in that previous efforts to explain variations in violence had mainly relied on structural variables such as the levels of urbanization and economic development.

Lijphart and Lehmbruch distinguish two main types of political decision-making. In the words of Lehmbruch (1974:97), these are:

AUTHORS' NOTE: *The contribution of Jürg Steiner to this paper was supported by a grant from the Swiss National Science Foundation* (Nationalfonds).

(a) The competitive pattern of conflict management (the fundamental device of which is the majority principle);

(b) The noncompetitive, "cartelized" pluralist pattern (which works by *amicabilis compositio,* "amicable agreement").

Instead of amicable agreement, Lijphart uses the term "consociational" decision-making, which we will use also in this paper. As Barry (1975) has correctly pointed out, there is some confusion in the literature about the terms consociationalism and consociational democracy. These terms are used interchangeably in a descriptive and in a theoretical sense. Descriptively they designate a particular type of decision-making; theoretically they refer to a complex theory stipulating the pattern of decision-making as a key variable. In this paper, we will speak of consociational *decision-making* if we mean the descriptive term, of consociational *theory* if we refer to the theoretical meaning of the term.

The consociational theory postulates that in countries which are subculturally strongly segmented, consociational decision-making is more likely to lead to peaceful relations among the subcultures than is competitive decision-making. Lijphart (1969:216) has embedded this central hypothesis into various other propositions. He mentions the following four facilitating conditions for consociational decision-making to be implemented:

(1) That the elites have the ability to accommodate the divergent interests and demands of the subcultures.

(2) This requires that they have the ability to transcend cleavages and to join in a common effort with the elites of rival subcultures.

(3) This in turn depends on their commitment to the maintenance of the system and to the improvement of its cohesion and stability.

(4) Finally, all of the above requirements are based on the assumption that the elites understand the perils of political fragmentation.

In a further step, Lijphart indicates preconditions under which the above four requirements are most likely to be fulfilled. These preconditions fall under three main headings. The first relates to inter-subcultural relations among elites. Lijphart argues that the following preconditions are conducive to consociational decision-making: (a) the existence of external threats to the country; (b) a multiple balance of power among the subcultures instead of either a dual balance or a clear hegemony by one subculture; (c) a relatively low total load on the decision-making apparatus. The second concerns inter-subcultural relations at the mass level; here the crucial precondition for consociational decision-making are distinct lines of cleavage among the subcultures. Finally, the third involves the elite-mass relations within the individual subcultures for which Lijphart enumerates the following favorable preconditions for consociational decision-making: (a) a high degree of internal political cohesion of the subcultures; (b) an adequate articulation of the interests of the subcultures; (c) a widespread approval of the principle of government by elite cartel. Besides preconditions of consociational decision-making, Lijphart's theory includes a side-effect of this particular mode of decision-making, namely "a certain degree of immobilism."

Lehmbruch did not spell out the consociational theory in the same detail. His major contribution, going beyond Lijphart, is his strong emphasis of the historical dimension. He gives great weight to the argument that consociational decision-making can only be understood if it is seen in its historical development. For Austria, Lehmbruch (1974:93) argues, for example, that

> Political parties continue to manage their conflicts according to those rules of the parliamentary game which (as for example the *Junktim*) were used in the Hapsburg Empire to establish the fragile modus vivendi of the different nations of the monarchy, and the political usages of the Republic still bear the impact of the politics of *Ausgleich*, that is, the settlement of ethnic antagonisms by institutional devices such as patronage, committees representing the different groups, demarcation of autonomous spheres of influence, and so on.

After Lijphart and Lehmbruch, quite a few other authors have contributed to the consociational theory so that one began to speak of a consociational school (Bluhm, 1973; Daalder, 1971; Huyse, 1970; Lorwin, 1971; McRae, 1974; Nordlinger, 1972; Powell, 1970; Stiefbold, 1974; Steiner, 1974). A good overview of this literature is offered in two review essays by Daalder (1974a) and Barry (1975) and a reader by McRae (1974). This paper is also a review essay, but it will differ from Daalder's and Barry's reviews. Whereas they have concentrated on a few major works of the consociational theory, we shall deal with a much broader literature. We will go back once more to the four countries from which the consociational theory originally developed: Switzerland, Austria, the Netherlands, and Belgium. Our question will be whether the historical development of these countries really supports the theory. To answer this question, we will look not only at the consociational literature but, as much as possible, at the whole literature that can throw some light on the historical development of these countries. This literature will include not only political science but also other disciplines such as history, sociology, and law.

We will conclude that the historical development in the four countries lends much less support to the consociational theory than was originally thought. This should make us careful about trying to "export" consociational decision-making to countries with a high level of hostility among their cultural groups. But we will also conclude that the cosociational theory has opened the path in the right direction; if further developed, it should have a great potential.

We will discuss one country after another, beginning with Switzerland. For each country, we will deal with four major issues. *The first issue is whether the country belongs to the theoretical universe to which the consociational theory applies.* As we have seen, this universe consists of all countries which are *subculturally strongly segmented.* Culturally relatively homogeneous countries are outside the universe since the problem which the consociational theory addresses does not exist in these countries. If a country is not divided in cultural groups, there is obviously no potential for violence among such groups. The literature shows that the distinction between subculturally segmented and nonsegmented countries is problematic. Thus, Barry (1975) and Germann (1975) argue, contrary to Lijphart and Lehmbruch, that Switzerland is culturally relatively homogeneous; according to this view, linguistic and religious affiliations have not led to the development of real subcultures. On the other hand, Barry accepts that Belgium has sufficiently strong subcultures to fall within the theoretical universe of the consociational theory. Part of the confusion is linked to the fact that *subcultural segmentation* is often not clearly enough distinguished from *cultural diversity.* By cultural diversity we mean simply that the members of a political system differ with regard to cultural attributes such as language, religion, and race. The people sharing the same cultural attribute may or may not develop a sense of identity that distinguishes them from other members of the system. We speak of subcultural segmentation only if such feelings of self-identification exist. Possible indicators are responses to attitudinal survey questions, frequency of interactions among the people sharing the same cultural attribute, and organizational ties among these people. We agree with Daalder (1974a: 615), who critically notes that "demographic variables are often assumed to be of attitudinal importance, with little investigation of the degree to which this is actually true." The task is then to determine whether, in Switzerland for example, the Catholics have such a sense of self-identification that they can be called a genuine subculture. We will see that this task cannot be easily resolved with the existing literature. Elegant mathematical formulas like the one developed by Rae and Taylor (1970) are of no help since they simply measure cultural diversity and not subcultural segmentation. A complicating factor is that we have to take account of a longitudinal dimension since a country can change from a segmented to a nonsegmented state and vice versa. For example, perhaps Austria was subculturally segmented in the 1950s but possibly this is not true today.

A second issue for each of the four countries is to determine whether the predominant decision-making mode can be characterized as consociational. Here again, we will have to consider possible changes over time. Lehmbruch (1974:91-92) distinguishes consociational decision-making from simple bargaining. In bargaining situations, the actors differ on transitive preferences; consequently "they may agree on a compromise which constitutes an intermediate point on a common preference scale. This is usually done by incremental concessions of the bargaining actors, and often it is assumed that the intermediate solution is a 'just,' 'natural,' or 'rational' one." With consociational decision-making, on the other hand,

> Preferences of the actors are incompatible and intransitive. Hence, there exists no common preference scale on which an intermediate solution may be found . . . the actors may agree on large-scale barter similar to package deals as they occur not infrequently in international negotiations; this procedure means that one of the actors offers a concession he detests in exchange for a concession by his opponent that the latter detests equally strongly. This formula, known in Austria under the name of *Junktim,* amounts to a partial realization of the actors' incompatible and intransitive preferences in different domains; its significant mark is that often there exists no objective relation among the "junctimized" *(junktimiert)* matters, and that the solution can be labeled neither "intermediate" nor "just" nor "natural."

For Lijphart (1969:213-214), "the grand coalition cabinet is the most typical and obvious, but not the only possible consociational solution." Advisory committees may be of great importance; Lijphart considers "the powerful Social and Economic Council of the Netherlands a perfect example of a cartel of economic elites." These committees may also be "ad hoc bodies, such as the cartels of top party leaders that negotiated the 'school pacts' in Holland in 1917 and in Belgium in 1958." According to Lijphart (1969:224), "the degree of competitive or cooperative behavior by elites must . . . be seen as a continuum." Most countries are said to have "some consociational features." As examples, Lijphart mentions the grand coalition in West Germany from 1966 till 1969, and in the United States, "after the Civil War, a consociational arrangement developed that gave to the Southern leaders—by such means as chairmanships of key Congressional committees and the filibuster—a crucial position in federal decision-making."

These definitional efforts seem to establish a good feeling of what is meant by consociational decision-making. But looking closely at the literature about our four countries, we will detect a lot of ambiguities. Thus, for example, it remains unclear to what extent the Austrian change in 1966 from a grand coalition to a one-party cabinet was a change from a consociational to a competitive pattern; some authors argue that only the tip of the iceberg had changed, while the basic decision-making structure remained the same. With regard to Switzerland, Barry (1975) stresses the competitive nature of the referendum, challenging the predominant view that Swiss decision-making is consociational. In the final section of this paper, we will argue that the distinction between competitive and consociational decision-making is too simple and that a more exhaustive typology has to be constructed.

As a third issue, we will have to ask for each country whether the relations among the subcultures are violent or peaceful. This seems a rather simple issue, since publications like the *World Handbook of Political and Social Indicators* (Taylor and Hudson, 1972) contain a fair amount of data about political violence. One problem with these data is that it remains often unclear whether they refer specifically to the relations among subcultures or to more general aspects of political violence. A much more severe problem is that such statistics usually deal only with manifest violence and leave aside the question of structural violence. Many listeners were shocked when Johan Galtung, in a recent lecture at the University of Zurich, described Switzerland as having a high level of structural violence. Using the term of symbolic violence, Ziegler (1976) has also challenged the notion that Switzerland is a peaceful country. The argument of Galtung and Ziegler is that Switzerland has a great deal of social inequality, with the lower strata being exploited by the higher strata. We agree that the concept of structural (or symbolic) violence draws our attention to an important phenomenon. In recent developments in South Africa, for example, not only the outbreak of actual violence was important but also the already previously existing structural violence. The consociational literature has not paid enough attention to the phenomenon of structural violence although not neglecting it completely. We shall argue in this paper that structural violence should be treated as a key variable in any decision-making theory. Conceptually, however, manifest and structural violence should be carefully distinguished. To make this distinction even clearer, we prefer the concept of social inequality to the concept of structural violence, reserving the term violence to manifest violence.

As a fourth and final issue, we will have to deal with the problem of causality for each country. Even if a country would be characterized by strong subcultural segmentation, consociational decision-making, and low levels of violence, this would not necessarily mean that consociational decision-making was the cause of the peaceful relations among the subcultures. The causal relationship could just be reversed in the sense that consociational decision-making would not be a cause but a consequence of low levels of violence. It might also be that the two variables have no direct causal relationship but depend on a third variable such as the level of economic prosperity or changes in the Catholic church. We will see that the exact nature of the causal relationships is often hard to determine on the basis of the existing literature.

2. SWITZERLAND

SUBCULTURAL SEGMENTATION

The Department of Political Science at the University of Geneva recently conducted the first broad, systematic analysis of Swiss cleavages, based on a national survey sample of the Swiss electorate in 1972 (Sidjanski et al., 1975). These data reveal interesting political differences among the groups formed by Swiss linguistic, religious, and class cleavages. For example, 30 percent of the French-speaking and 16 percent of German-speaking Swiss consider themselves primarily as members of their linguistic group rather than as members of their canton or nation.[1] Although there are no linguistic parties, language differences, as demonstrated by Kerr (1974), have a bearing on voters' preferences; controlling for religion and class, he found that French-speaking Swiss are more sympathetic to the parties of the left than the German-speaking Swiss.

The survey did not establish the degree to which the Swiss consider themselves members of their religious groups. But clear differences in partisan choice were revealed; practicing Catholics tend to support the Christian Democrats, while nonpracticing Catholics and Protestants are more likely to vote for the other major parties—the Free-Democrats, the Social-Democrats, and the Swiss People's party. A link between social class and partisan choice was also established; not surprisingly, manual workers vote most often for the Social Democratic party.

The three cleavages crosscut one another. The relative importance of the cleavages as well as their crosscutting structure vary considerably from one canton to another. For many substantive issues the cleavages are politically salient at the cantonal rather than at the national level. For example, in Fribourg, a predominantly Catholic canton, Protestants form a cohesive subculture with their own interests, identities, and organizational ties. They take an active part in cantonal politics, especially on the question of the religious orientation of the schools. In the national arena, however, many of the Protestant Fribourgeois identify more as members of their canton than as members of their religious group because religious issues are not particularly salient in Swiss national politics. There are many impressionistic studies of Swiss subcultures (Weilenmann, 1951). But nobody has as yet undertaken a systematic study to determine the precise number and relative strengths of the subcultures at the cantonal and national levels. For now we can only state that the Swiss subcultural structure is extremely complex; a great number of actors engage in subcultural confrontation in the cantonal and national arenas.

The Geneva survey also offers age-cohort data which allow an assessment of how groups' identities and partisan choices have varied over time. These data suggest that the ties between the individual and his linguistic and religious group may have declined; and this, in turn, may indicate a more general decline in the degree of subcultural segmentation. Among younger, and especially Catholic voters, religion and religiosity are less salient considerations in their party preferences. Language differences, which were particularly important for the generation which reached political maturity during the First World War, are likewise a less prominent determinant of political choice. The impact of class differences, on the other hand, has remained fairly constant over several generations. The survey also revealed that the sense of national identity among the Swiss has become more prevalent. Among French-speakers, for example, only 31 percent of the oldest age cohort, but 55 percent of the youngest, think of themselves primarily as Swiss.

Is Switzerland still subculturally strongly segmented or has it become a relatively homogeneous country? There is no easy answer because no yardsticks exist; as said earlier, there is no simple computation formula for subcultural segmentation similar to the one Rae and Taylor (1970) have developed for cultural diversity. The reason for this lack of a commonly accepted yardstick is, of course, that it is much more difficult to measure the level of subcultural segmentation than to assay the level of cultural diversity. If we wanted to determine, for example, whether subcultural segmentation was greater among Dutch Catholics than Swiss Catholics, simple attitudinal survey questions would not be sufficient; we would also have to consider the interaction patterns and the organizational links within the two subcultures. It would be even more difficult to compare, for example, the Austrian "Lager" with the Swiss language groups, since the social bases of the subcultures would be different.

In view of these difficult problems of measurement, we cannot expect more precision than is actually possible. The best solution in this situation seems to be a well informed expert judgment, along the lines of Lorwin's (1971) elegant analysis. This method raises, of course, problems of reliability, but it may better fulfill the criterion of validity. Without pretense of too much precision, our conclusion is that among the European democracies Switzerland ranks neither with the very homogeneous nor with the very segmented systems. Thus, Switzerland seems a marginal case for the application of the consociational theory; it is certainly not a hard test for the theory.

DECISION-MAKING

The most outstanding and incontestable sign of elite accommodation is the composition of the collegial Swiss executive, the Federal Council, which is elected for the full legislative period of four years without possibility of a vote of nonconfidence. The Federal Council includes members of the four major political parties: the Christian Democrats, the Free Democrats, and the Social Democrats each have two representatives on the Council, and the Swiss People's Party has one representative. This allocation of positions on the Council is roughly proportional to the parties' share of the popular vote. Given the size of the Federal Council, no other party is entitled to a seat based on its share of the popular vote. The practice of having all or most major parties represented in the Council has a long tradition in Swiss political history. The last step was taken in 1959 when the Social Democrats were accorded a proportionate share of seats.[2] Efforts are also taken to have the "appropriate" mix of linguistic, religious, and cantonal representatives. If one of the three largest parties, for example, has already nominated a French-speaking candidate, the second candidate must almost necessarily be German-speaking. A balanced distribution of linguistic, religious, and cantonal affiliations is sought not only within each party but also for the Federal Council as a whole. Hence, in the allocation of positions on the Federal Council, efforts are made to include representatives of the largest parties and also representatives of the various subcultures in Swiss society (Gruner, 1967).

This spirit of accommodation mirrored in the distribution of seats on the Federal Council may spill over into the formulation of public policy. Indeed, numerous studies of Swiss decision-making underline the willingness of Swiss political leaders to compromise in order to avoid conflict

(Gruner, 1969; Lehmbruch, 1967; Neidhart, 1970; Sidjanski, 1974). Urio's (1972) study of the so-called Mirage affair is especially useful for it shows how consociational decision-making can prevail, even when an issue fosters considerable conflict. Urio relates how in preparing to purchase 100 French Mirage fighters, the federal government made several mistakes which inflated originally anticipated costs. The bungling nurtured suspicion; there were even complaints that the Parliament had not always been told the truth. Opposition to the proposed purchase was vigorous. At one point tensions became so great that the Social Democrats demanded the resignation of the Free-Democratic Federal Councillor responsible for national defense. Despite these difficulties, the Swiss political leaders managed to come up with a solution whereby 57 of the proposed 100 fighters were purchased. Accepted almost unanimously by Parliament, this solution represented a compromise between those who insisted on the purchase of 100 planes and those who wanted to renounce the whole deal. Though elite accommodation prevailed, the compromise ironically meant that the Swiss had to pay more for each of the planes bought from France.

But such compromises are common also among political systems that are not normally considered consociational. Moreover, there are several features of the Swiss decision-making process that do not conform to the consociational model of decision-making.

(1) The Swiss parties that are partners in the Federal Council do not formally agree to support an articulated set of policies. Until 1967, policy issues were never formally discussed by the Swiss coalition partners. For the legislative period 1967-1971, the Federal Council, for the first time, formulated a paper containing "guidelines" for governmental activities. These "guidelines" were not nearly as formal as platforms developed in other political settings. They were negotiated, not by the government parties, but rather by the Federal Councillors after they had been elected for a four-year term. The guidelines were not binding; after four years the legislature discussed a report issued by the Federal Council on the fulfillment of the guidelines; but the legislature had no sanctions to indicate their satisfaction with the report. After the 1971 election, the government parties themselves agreed on a set of policies to be implemented in the coming session; but these policies were formulated in such a general and vague way, that their actual significance was minimal. After the 1975 election, the government parties gave up the idea to write down an agreement on policy goals. The Federal Council, however, formulated again guidelines for its governmental activities. The point here is that no specially articulated consensus on Swiss public policy exists among the major national political parties. Any agreement that emerges takes place on a rather ad hoc basis.

(2) While there is agreement concerning the party distribution in the Federal Council, there is no agreement among the major parties concerning the particular individuals who should be elected to the Federal Council. The candidates are presented to the Federal Assembly (both houses of Parliament meeting in a joint session) by the individual parties and not by the government coalition as a whole. There have been quite a few cases when the candidate supported by a particular party was *not* elected by the Federal Assembly. This usually happens because the party nominates a candidate from one of its extreme factions and, therefore, the other parties do not consider the nominee acceptable. In 1959, for example, the Social Democrats nominated Walther Bringolf, fully aware that his Communist past might present problems. Indeed, Bringolf did not get the absolute majority of the votes in the Federal Assembly. The other parties proceeded to elect Hanspeter Tschudi, a more acceptable Social Democrat.

(3) Just as Swiss political leaders avoid conflict through compromise, there are instances when compromises are not reached and decisions are either made through non-consociational means or are not made at all (Hughes, 1962; Jenny, 1966; Kocher, 1967). Disagreement among Swiss political leaders is not uncommon. Since the deliberations and votes in the Federal Council are secret, it is not possible to ascertain the degree of consensus among the councillors. But parliamentary sessions are open and therefore the disagreement within and among parties as well as the conflicts between Parliament and the Federal Council are visible. One example of the conflict between the Federal Council and the Parliament, which took place in the 1966-1967 winter, is described by Peter Gilg (1969). The federation was confronted with the delicate task of bringing its financial affairs back into balance. In the Federal Council a compromise was reached; the tax on stock dividends would be retained, and in return for this, a 10 percent increase in income and sales tax was scheduled. In the parliamentary deliberations, a number of members of the three bourgeois government parties opposed the stock dividend tax; consequently it was abolished despite the recommendation of the Federal Council. The Social Democrats opposed the increase in income and sales tax as a countermove that led to the fall of that part of the government compromise, too. Such independent actions of the Parliament are not uncommon in Switzerland.

(4) The existence of a referendum procedure also undermines the consociational character of the decision-making process. Many key policy issues in Switzerland are decided through the referendum; and by its very character, the referendum is an institution that permits a majority to impose its solution on the minority. It should be noted, however, that the

referendum is essentially a process of mass and not elite decision-making; the consociational theory is explicitly concerned with elite—not mass—decision-making. Yet is is also true that the referendum is important for the resolution of conflicts among the government parties; if no solution can be found in the Federal Council or in Parliament, the conflict is often settled through the referendum. Over the question of health insurance, for example, the Social Democrats were so far apart from the other coalition parties that no solution within the government was feasible. Hence the issue was resolved by the referendum.

The preceding discussion suggests that since the Swiss decision-making process includes consociational as well as non-consociational elements, it is not a simple matter to categorize the Swiss system according to the conventional typology offered by proponents of the consociational school. It is particularly unclear what weight should be given to the different elements of the decision-making process. For example, how much should the existence of a grand coalition count—as against the competition of the parties in referenda?

VIOLENCE

Switzerland's reputation for peaceful relations among its subcultures is confirmed by the data reported by the *World Handbook of Political and Social Indicators* (Taylor and Hudson, 1972). Between 1948 and 1967, domestic political violence caused no deaths in Switzerland; only 15 other nations, including the Netherlands, had such an impressive record. During the same period domestic violence in Belgium and Austria produced 10 and six deaths respectively. Over the same two decades, Switzerland experienced seven armed attacks and four riots; Belgium and Austria were plagued by considerably more and the Netherlands by slightly more domestic violence.

The absence of subcultural hostility has been taken so much for granted that no one has bothered to conduct a systematic study of the subject. The Année Politique Suisse (1965-) which, among other things, provides annual summaries of linguistic and religious affairs, has reported sporadic hostilities; but the overall impression one draws from this source is that subcultural peace prevails.

In this context it is important to note that a frequent precondition of hostility—*relative deprivation*—is remarkably absent among Swiss language groups. Glass (1975) has demonstrated that the minority language groups do not feel more deprived than the German-speaking Swiss. This is an interesting finding because one may have expected that the stronger leftist tendencies in the French-speaking area would indicate a higher sense of deprivation.

The Jura problem represents the most notable exception to Swiss tranquility, and it has precipitated most of the limited violence that has ruffled the Swiss over the past decades. Henecka (1972) offers the most thorough analysis of the Jura conflict (see also Mayer, 1969; Keech, 1972; Forster et al., 1074). The Berne canton comprises a German-speaking majority and a predominantly French-speaking minority of the Jura districts.[3] The French-speaking minority is further divided between the predominantly Catholic population of the North Jura districts and the predominantly Protestant population of the South Jura districts while the remainder of the canton is predominantly Protestant. Since the late 1940s, the French-speaking Catholics in particular have actively sought greater autonomy from the Berne canton as a means to free themselves from what they considered the political and economic hegemony of the German-speaking majority. To attract attention to their cause, the Jura separatists have occasionally resorted to violence and sabotage; though negligible in contrast to subcultural strife in the United States or Northern Ireland, this violence was frightening to the Swiss, who are accustomed to order and civility. Efforts to resolve the conflict through elite conciliation have not been successful; separatists and Bernese leaders have been unable to negotiate acceptable compromises.

Tensions between the indigenous population and the foreign workers have been another source of severe political conflict. Since the early 1960s, there has been a tremendous influx of foreign workers into Switzerland to fill the unskilled and semi-skilled positions in the labor force that have been shunned by the Swiss. Coming primarily from southern European countries, they now number about one million in a total Swiss population of six million. Hoffmann-Nowotny (1973) analyzes carefully how the Swiss have become increasingly particularistic and ethnocentric as the community of foreign workers has expanded; and, consequently, how the foreign workers have been socially isolated and subjected to various forms of discrimination. Anxieties over increasing immigration have encouraged the formation of two anti-alien parties which have demanded restrictions of the number of foreign workers permitted in Switzerland. Once again, elite accommodation failed to avert conflict. In 1970, and again in 1974, anti-alien initiatives, which were, however, defeated in referenda, badly split the indigenous population.

Theoretical Interpretations

The overview of recent developments with regard to subcultural segmentation, decision-making patterns, and hostility shows that Switzerland does *not* neatly fit the classical formulation of the consociational theory. Hostility is the least problematic variable; if we do not take account of structural violence, Switzerland appears, indeed, as one of the most peaceful countries in the world.

Whether political decision-making in Switzerland can be characterized as consociational depends on the definition of the concept. If the term is narrowly defined, delimiting only situations where all participants explicitly agree to a common solution, consociational decision-making seems to be relatively infrequent in Switzerland.

For the consociational theory to apply to Switzerland, it must also be demonstrated that Swiss society is subculturally strongly segmented. With its four languages and two major religions, Switzerland has certainly a strong cultural diversity. But this is not identical with saying that Switzerland has strong subcultures with intense feelings of self-identity. There are indeed some data showing that *national* identification is increasing and *subcultural* segmentation decreasing in Switzerland. For the time being, however, it still seems that Switzerland belongs, if only marginally, to the theoretical universe with which the consociational theory is concerned.

Let us now assume that Switzerland is subculturally sufficiently segmented for the theory to apply, that its decision-making can be characterized in a broad sense as consociational, and that we exclude structural violence so that Switzerland appears as a relatively peaceful country. If these three conditions hold, does this necessarily mean that the consociational theory is supported? The answer seems to be no. To be sure, the consociational theory would give a plausible explanation for the Swiss situation but certainly not the *only* plausible one. One could also argue that consociational decision-making is not the *cause* but the *consequence* of a low level of hostility. According to this interpretation, consociational decision-making would be a simple epiphenomenon. This would leave us with the task to look for other causes of the low hostility. There are some that come immediately to mind. The high *economic development* of Switzerland may have satisfied the demands of the various subcultures to such an extent that no strong feelings of relative deprivation arose. It may also be important that the three major languages have about the same international *prestige*. This is, for example, not the case in Belgium, where the uneven international prestige of the two major languages is said to have contributed to many of the current problems. A third cause for the low hostility in Switzerland may be that the load on the central system is not very heavy. Because of the *federal structure*, many of the tricky problems for a subcultural country are dealt with primarily at the cantonal and even at the local level. *Neutrality*, too, takes away many problems from the central political arena. This short discussion shows that there are other plausible explanations besides consociational decision-making for the low level of hostility in Switzerland. This does not, of course, exclude consociational decision-making as an explanatory factor. But it indicates that the simultaneous appearance of consociational decision-making and a low level of hostility does not necessarily mean that the latter is a consequence of the former.

The problem of causality may be further elucidated if we take a closer look at the violence that occurred in connection with the Jura problem. Its evolution is compatible with the classical formulation of the consociational theory. The Bernese government has tried for many years to solve the problem in a consociational way. It has, for example, invited the separatists to participate in an expert committee. The hope was that this committee would find a solution acceptable to all participants. But the separatists have again and again rejected such invitations. When the consociational method failed, the Bernese government tried to use the majority principle to find a solution. A constitutional amendment of March 1970 opened the way for a whole series of referenda. In a first referendum, in June 1974, a slight majority of the Jura population decided to form their own canton. But the constitutional amendment gave the districts which opted against the canton Jura the opportunity to say in a second referendum whether they wanted to stay with the canton Berne. In March 1975, the southern Protestant districts decided to remain with the canton Berne. In September 1975, some border communities could decide in still another referendum whether they wanted to change the district. In a last step a national referendum will have to decide whether Article 2 of the federal constitution, which enumerates the cantons, shall be changed to add the canton Jura.

This majoritarian procedure with a whole series of referenda has probably not brought the Jura problem closer to a solution. Hostility is even on the increase; there is a strong possibility that the solution that has come out of the referenda will be further contested. Thus, the separatists say openly that they will never give up their claim to the southern districts.

From a theoretical view one may argue that the development of the Jura problem fits the consociational theory. The fact that the leaders on both sides have not firmly chosen a consociational strategy could explain why the hostility has not decreased. But there is also another perspective: perhaps a consociational strategy was not possible because hostility was too high. There would be ways to explain the high hostility without referring to the lack of consociational decision-making. It may be important that the Northern Jura, where the separatists have their stronghold, is in several ways in a minority position within the canton Bern. Unlike the Southern Jura, the Northern Jura is not only linguistically, but also religiously in a clear minority position. Furthermore, the Northern Jura counts economically among the weakest regions of the canton. This minority situation could explain why feelings of relative deprivation and even hostility have developed in the Northern Jura.

The general discussion of the possible causal relation between consociational decision-making and the level of hostility is further complicated because some authors claim that in the long run consociational decision-making may contribute to malaise and even hostility. This argument is most forcefully put forward by Germann (1975). According to his view, consociational decision-making is very damaging to the innovation capacity of a political system, since the process is very slow and the most conservative group always has a veto power. Germann also complains that elite cooperation prohibits the citizens from casting instrumental votes, for they are unable to replace one set of leaders with another. The lack of innovation and meaningful political participation cause, following the analysis of Germann, frustrations on the part of the citizens. These frustrations may ultimately lead to the outbreak of violence. Germann argues that if Switzerland shifted to a two-party system, modeled after the Anglo-Saxon pattern, with periodic changes in power, the system's innovative capacity would be bolstered and Swiss citizens could play more efficacious political roles. To foster the development of a two-party system organized around class divisions, he proposes a new electoral system, a full-time Parliament, and restrictions on the use of referenda. Germann does not fear that the introduction of a competitive, majoritarian system would jeopardize subcultural concord since, in his view, the growing homogeneity of Swiss culture precludes the danger that greater political competition would turn one subculture against another.

There are some empirical data which can be used in support of Germann's thesis. In a recent national survey, Inglehart and Sidjanski (1974) found a diffuse sense of frustration among the Swiss population. They determined that a rather large segment of the population disagrees with the establishment on such key issues as relations with the European

Community, entry into the United Nations, the political role of women, and the desirability of foreign workers. While this dissatisfaction has not yet altered the traditional parties' rather stable electoral following, it has affected the outcome of referenda. Proposals supported by the traditional parties have recently been relatively often defeated or barely accepted. This dissent has had conservative overtones; accordingly, Inglehart and Sidjanski have labelled members of the discontented groups as anti-establishment traditionalists.

Imboden (1964) too noticed growing frustrations; as early as 1964 he spoke of a "Malaise Helvétique," an expression that has been widely used since then. An obvious argument against linking this "Malaise Helvétique" with consociational decision-making is that in countries without consociationalism, such as France and Italy, frustrations may be even greater. In such comparisons, however, many variables are not held constant. Thus, it may be that the level of frustration in France and Italy might be far greater if these countries practiced consociational decision-making.

In sum, the Swiss case does not disprove the consociational theory; but neither does it confirm it in a convincing manner, for alternative and equally plausible interpretations are possible.

3. AUSTRIA

THE DISSOLUTION OF THE GREAT COALITION IN 1966

In the aftermath of the Second World War, Austrian political leaders abandoned their long tradition of internecine struggles in order to pursue a more conciliatory political course. Accordingly, from 1945 to 1966 the two largest political parties—the Austrian People's Party (OeVP) and the Socialist Party of Austria (SPOe)—which together have never won less than 83 percent of the vote in any postwar parliamentary election, formed one great coalition after another. Government by great coalition precluded conventional forms of parliamentary opposition and required widespread elite consensus. Government by great coalitions also meant that such tangible political rewards as cabinet and bureaucratic posts were scrupulously allocated between the coalition partners. These successive great coalitions, so most observers have maintained, facilitated Austria's postwar economic recovery and social integration.

It was somewhat surprising, then, when rule by great coalition ended suddenly following the 1966 parliamentary elections. In 1966, the OeVP formed Austria's first postwar one-party government. And since 1970 the

SPOe has led successive one-party governments.[4] Thus Austria constitutes a case in which the institutional trappings of consociationalism were replaced by a more majoritarian pattern.

Students of Austrian politics do not concur as to whether the 1966 demise of the great coalition was simply a change in political form or whether it represented a substantial alteration in the distribution of political authority and the decision-making processes. On one extreme, Stiefbold (1974:121) claims that the "dissolution of the Great Coalition in 1966 amounted to a change not merely of governments but, to a great extent, also of regimes." Steiner (1972:418-419), on the other hand, supports the view that while the Austrian elite has evolved toward more competitive relations, the 1966 shift "did not involve an abrupt change in elite behavior;" he further quotes approvingly a high-ranking Socialist politician who commented in a 1968 interview that "only the shape of the top of the iceberg—the composition of the cabinet—had been altered." Along this line, Lehmbruch (1971) notes that the spirit of accommodation between the coalition partners had begun to erode in the early 1960s; he observes that prior to 1966, the OeVP and SPOe often practiced "Bereichsopposition" whereas since 1966 they have frequently engaged in "Bereichskoalition."[5] That elite cooperation has survived one-party cabinets is suggested by Fischer (1973) who has demonstrated that between 1966 and 1973 about 80 percent of all parliamentary votes, including many on key foreign policy and economic issues, were unanimous, though the non-unanimous votes often concerned key decisions in such areas as educational policy. There are several other indicators that suggest the persistence of consociational decision-making: great coalitions are still common among the Länder governments; the major economic interest groups continue to display a remarkable consensus and willingness to compromise (Pelinka, 1973; Gerlich, 1972); one-party governments have not markedly departed from the application of proporz in the bureaucracies (Kneucker, 1973).

While the literature offers little empirical data or explicitly articulated criteria to help judge precisely changes in Austrian elite behavior, one comes away with the impression that since the early 1960s Austrian political leaders have gravitated slightly toward a more competitive stance and that the move in 1966 from great coalitions to one-party governments was merely an institutional expression of this evolution. Welan (1975) perceptively distinguishes elite behavior in the public and non-public arenas. He argues that while cooperation between the leaders of the two largest parties has continued since 1966 in the non-public arena, in the public arena a change to a more competitive behavior pattern has taken place. Thus basically the same political actors play different games in different arenas.

SUBCULTURAL SEGMENTATION AND HOSTILITY
BETWEEN THE SUBCULTURES

Austria's major subcultures, termed "Lager," are the Socialist (red) and Catholic (black) worlds. On the basis of 1968 and 1973 national surveys, Engelmann and Schwartz (1974a, 1974b) indicate that the Socialist camp includes primarily urban (and especially Viennese) blue-collar workers who attend Church infrequently or not at all while the Catholic camp comprises primarily practicing Catholics from small towns and rural areas who are farmers or who are drawn from middle-class occupations. The red-black dichotomy refers to more than differences in partisan choices; it represents a distinction in general perspectives and defines individuals socially and economically as well as politically. Each of the two "Lager" has close organizational ties, ranging from the party organization to professional and recreational activities.

Subcultural enmity has plagued modern Austrian politics. It erupted into open and bloody civil war in the early 1930s and precipitated the fall of the First Austrian Republic. Given this stormy and violent tradition, the decline in subcultural segmentation and hostility and the concomitant political calm that are described for the time after 1945 seem particularly striking. In summarizing the views of most observers, Steiner (1972:272-273) notes that while in 1945 "each Lager continued to doubt the democratic convictions and trust-worthiness of the other Lager," as the postwar period unfolded "the rigidity and intensity of Lager partisanship is seen to decline."

There are two problems with the studies dealing with postwar Austrian subcultural relations. First, they do not distinguish clearly between individuals who identify as members of a subculture and individuals of a subculture who have hostile feelings or who act hostilely toward members of another subculture. For Powell (1970:37) the displeasure expressed by parents over the prospect that their child may marry a member of an opposing subculture is a sign of subcultural hostility. While this may be the case in many instances, it is also plausible to interpret this displeasure as a desire to perpetuate the family's ties to the subculture and, in more general terms, to sustain the viability of the subculture. Steiner (1972:183) defines Lagermentality as "thinking in terms of hostile camps." Such a definition, we contend, inappropriately precludes the possibility that individuals may identify strongly with a particular subculture without harboring animosity toward the members of other subcultures.

A second difficulty is that the literature offers hardly any empirical data to support the proposition that subcultural segmentation and hostility have declined. Since there are no pertinent survey data for the early postwar period, assertions regarding the waning of subcultural segmentation and enmity must be chiefly impressionistic. With regard to psychological hostility some data are available beginning with the 1960s. For this period hostility seems to be at a rather low level. In his 1967 study of the city of Hallein, Powell (1970:38) asked whether a government controlled by the other Lager "would ever seriously endanger the welfare of the country." Even among those with a cumulative cleavage position—those respondents separated along religious, class, and party lines—only 20 percent of the OeVP and 25 percent of the SPOe respondents indicated concern. Powell concludes that "the absolute numbers of hostile individuals are not large."

Stiefbold (1974:145, 176) in a more oblique fashion, also argues that subcultural hostility is low. He maintains that in order to sustain the cohesiveness of their respective subcultures, political elites adopted militant, highly ideological electoral strategies which tended to repolarize the political process. In pursuing such strategies, the elites, Stiefbold avers, "may have artificially prolonged the life of crisis-consociational rule beyond any 'objective' necessity." For Stiefbold, the "unbelievably smooth transition to a working governemnt-opposition model" suggests that subcultural hositility among the masses declined prior to the dissolution of the great coalition. Finally, data presented in the *World Handbook* (Taylor and Hudson, 1972) indicate a decline in hostile behavior. None of the six deaths caused by domestic violence has occurred since 1954 and only six of the 25 armed attacks and three of the 36 riots have taken place since 1960. Of course, for our purposes, these data are not entirely adequate since we do not know to what extent the reported hostile behavior is linked to subcultural disputes.

The decrease of hostility between the subcultures does not necessarily mean that the intensity of subcultural segmentation—in the sense of identities and organizational ties—has also decreased. It is often claimed in the literature that such a decrease has indeed taken place, but usually very little empirical support is given for such a claim. Most authors seem to assume that the intensity of subcultural segmentation must have declined if hostility between the subcultures has decreased. As we have argued before, this is an empirical question that may not be resolved a priori. The best data on the degree of subcultural segmentation can be found in the

1968 and 1973 national surveys of Engelmann and Schwartz (1974a, 1974b). They found that subcultural segmentation has persisted to a certain extent. They show, for example, that the political environment for consistent OeVP and SPOe voters is quite homogeneous; (homogeneity is defined as "identical political persuasion of majority of family, friends and work colleagues"). But they also present data which suggest the possible erosion of subcultural segmentation: for instance, more than a third of their respondents (37 percent) failed to vote for the same party in the four national elections between 1959 and 1966. Based on available sources, then, one can conclude that while Austria may still be to a certain extent subculturally segmented, subcultural hostility has been quite limited over the past decade.

Theoretical Interpretations

For Austria, as for Switzerland, the causal connections between elite accommodation and low levels of subcultural hostility cannot be con- clusively established. In his study, *Building an Austrian Nation,* Bluhm (1973:62) asserts that consociational decision-making has helped to create peaceful relations between the subcultures. He indicates that while Lager hostility was still pronounced in 1945, relations among political leaders were far more conciliatory than they had been during the First Republic. Stressing the significance of traumatic adult socialization he ascribes this change to the fact that many postwar Austrian leaders had "suffered a common persecution under the Nazis, either in their persons or in the persons of close friends and party comrades, and this counted for a great deal of promoting mutual tolerance, respect and even affection." While recognizing their basic differences in political values, the leaders of the rival Lager, according to Bluhm, were still willing to resolve pressing issues through compromises; he terms this spirit of cooperation "pragmatism of dissensus." Elite accommodation so effectively fostered social integration, he contends, that by the mid-1960s Austrian society had become subculturally relatively homogeneous.

But on the basis of our reading of the literature, this interpretation raises several difficulties. First, the existence of subcultural enmity in 1945 is assumed but never convincingly documented. Perhaps the common wartime suffering had salutary effects on subcultural relations at the mass as well as the elite levels. Perhaps most Austrian people shared the leaders' conviction that given the imperative of economic reconstruction, as well as the country's precarious international position, internal solidarity was essential. Second, that subcultural hostility has been so much more limited in the Second than in the First Austrian Republic may be attributed to changes other than those in the style of decision-making. Thus Bluhm recognizes the contribution that postwar economic development has made in establishing the necessary social and psychological bases for stable liberal democracy. But he argues further that consociational decision-making facilitated the economic miracle which eventually made the great coalition obsolete. But Bluhm fails to demonstrate persuasively that the Austrian economic recovery would not have occurred in the absence of consociational decision-making; after all, the postwar economic boom took place in other European countries—such as France and West Germany—where majoritarian practices prevailed.

Furthermore, Gerlich (1972) and Zapotoczky (1972) note that a decline in religiosity may explain why the traditional conflict between Catholics and anti-clerics is no longer a pressing political issue. Also, in Austria, as in other highly industrialized societies, a more complex social stratification system, highlighted by a growing, diversified middle-class as well as a more heterogeneous working class, has developed over the past generations. The simple class dichotomy mirrored in the traditional Lager, argue Bodzenta and Freytag (1972) has become less relevant to Austrian politics; consequently many contemporary social issues cut across rather than between the Lager. These considerations suggest that perhaps too much stress has been placed on the role of elite accommodation in establishing the political calm of postwar Austria.

According to such observers as Bluhm (1973), Nassmacher (1968), and Vodopivec (1966), consociational decision-making, regardless of its impact on subcultural relations, may induce the kind of political stagnation and malaise that concern the Swiss. Bluhm (1973:98) writes:

> Modern, changing Austria wanted a reform of the coalition system of government, which had earned a reputation for stalemate, inefficiency, and corruption and appeared to be a hopelessly outdated instrument for leading Austria toward further economic and social progress.

Complaints about political stalemate became less common following the termination of the great coalition: indeed, by 1968, Nassmacher (1968:145-146) already had noticed that the regime had become more flexible and responsive. But Gerlich (1972), among others, still complained about the lingering unnecessary remnants of consociational decision-making. Steiner (1972:167), on the other hand, suggests that the negative influence of consociational decision-making "was probably exaggerated by writers who opposed the Great Coalition and projected their own feelings on the public at large." In the absence of more rigorous analyses, no definitive conclusions can be reached regarding whether Austrian coalition politics had indeed produced stagnation and inefficiency.

4. THE NETHERLANDS

CHANGES IN THE SOCIAL BASES OF DUTCH POLITICS

Religious and class differences are the bases of the four major Dutch subcultures—Catholic, Calvinist, Socialist, and Liberal. Even more than in Switzerland or Austria, these subcultures—or pillars or blocs—as described by Kruijt (1959), Goudsblom (1967), Daalder (1966), and Lijphart (1975), have established networks of sectarian organizations to mobilize and serve their followers in nearly every facet of public life. The pervasiveness of bloc organizations has helped to nurture a sense of distance and isolation among the blocs as well as encouraging internal bloc cohesion; thus Lijphart (1975) and Gadourek (1961) offer data to demonstrate that the Dutch tend to marry and choose friends within and not across subcultures.

Until the 1960s the political parties representing the major pillars dominated Dutch politics.[6] But recently, several changes in the social bases of Dutch politics have altered the blocs and challenged their political hegemony. *The first, and perhaps most important change, is that subcultural solidarity along the confessional dimension, and most notably among Catholics, has waned visibly.* In his analysis of Dutch Catholicism, Thurlings (1971a, 1971b) documents the growing disenchantment among Catholic officials and practicing Catholics.[7] Thurlings sees this disenchantment rooted in the evolving status of Catholics in Dutch society. As a socially vulnerable minority in the 1860s, Dutch Catholics developed what Thurlings terms a defensive strategy to affirm their distinct identity and to protect and perpetuate their values by forming multiple social and political organizations. But by the 1960s, Thurlings continues, this defensive strategy and its concomitant institutional infrastructure had become increasingly superfluous to Catholics who, though not a majority, outnumbered Calvinists and the "unchurchables" and who had assumed prominent positions throughout Dutch society. Socially secure Catholics began to question the need for social isolation, and, gradually, the link between Catholics and certain institutional trappings of the Catholic subculture began to erode.[8]

This erosion, as Van Kemenade (1968) argues, has had a differentiated impact on Catholic organizations. He suggests that those organizations whose purposes include religious socialization—for example, elementary schools—have been relatively immune to the effects of deconfessionalization.[9] But those organizations whose primary purposes are to isolate Catholics and to breed an in-group mentality—for example, sports and social clubs—have been most deleteriously affected, most notably by declining membership, by the malaise among Catholics. As one such organization, the Catholic Party (KVP) has been especially hard-hit by deconfessionalization. For those Catholics who have loosened their ties with the Catholic bloc, religious affinities no longer mold partisan choices. But even more important is the growing number of practicing Catholics who, having shed their feeling of minority status, no longer feel obligated to vote for the KVP; they no longer feel compelled to find a political expression for their religious loyalty. Thus the percentage of Catholics voting for the KVP dropped from 83.5 percent in 1963 to just 38 percent in 1972 (DeBruyn, 1972). In addition, there are as many practicing as non-practicing Catholics among the supporters of the non-confessional Socialist Party (see Van den Berg and Molleman, 1974). Not surprisingly the KVP's share of the popular vote plummeted from 31.7 percent to 17 percent between 1963 and 1972.[10]

A second change has been the proliferation of splinter parties.[11] In every parliamentary election since 1963 a new party has surfaced to challenge the right of the bloc parties to perpetuate their monopolistic control over Dutch government; in 1972 these parties together captured nearly 16 percent of the popular vote. The multiplication of splinter parties may have been due in part to a growing dissatisfaction with the quality of Dutch democracy. Kuypers (1967) and Glastra van Loon (1967-1968) complain that the multiplicity of parties, the cumbersome and lengthy process of coalition formation, and the inherent conservatism of established political leaders has effectively deprived the Dutch voters of the right to alter, through the electoral process, the form and substance of their government. To make the government more responsive to the people, they argue, the Dutch should emulate the majoritarian Anglo-Saxon model.

There are also signs of popular discontent. According to national survey findings between 1967 and 1971 reported by Noordzij (1972), the proportion of respondents claiming that they had much influence as voters dropped from 48 percent to 19 percent. It should be noted, however, that only one splinter party—the Democrats '66—had as its primary goal the reform of the political system, and its electoral success was quite transient.[12] Furthermore, the supporters of the splinter parties, according to a survey analysis conducted by DeBruyn (1972), are more concerned with particular issues and policies than with the overall performance of the system. Noordzij (1972) also notes that only the voters of two of the splinter parties display an above average concern with the limited influence exercised by Dutch voters.

The third major change is that while religious issues have become politically less prominent, labor-management and intergenerational relations have become more polarized. As indicated by Windmuller (1969) and Peper (1973), until the late 1950s trade union leaders accepted a national wage policy which they hoped would spur postwar economic recovery by granting workers only modest annual pay increments, pegged to increases in the cost of living.[13] But as the postwar prosperity appeared more permanent, more and more workers became disenchanted with the failure of their leaders to assume a more militant position at the bargaining table. Workers began to demand more than cost of living increases; they wanted to share the prosperity; wildcat strikes became more common; the level of industrial disputes soared;[14] workers' militancy gradually forced national union leaders to harden their bargaining positions. Consequently, competition gradually replaced cooperation in labor-management relations.

Besides the increased tensions in labor-management relations, the Dutch have been troubled by greater intergenerational conflict as mirrored in the provo movement of the 1960s (see Van den Berg and Molleman, 1974) and, more recently, in a sharp rise in student unrest, especially at the University of Amsterdam. Drawing on the work of Mason (1974), Daalder (1974b), and Lijphart (1975), it is clear that the young Dutch radicals—the New Left—differ from the supporters of the Democrats '66 in several key respects. First, their attack on Dutch society has been broader and more profound; since they have challenged the basic values and authority patterns of Dutch society they would not have been appeased if the proposals proffered by the Democrats '66 for enhancing the quality of Dutch democracy had been enacted. Second, they have been more inclined to engage in civil disobedience to further their ends; disruptions of classes and occupations of university buildings have become more prevalent. Third, rather than trying to wield political influence by forming a new political party, they have acted, with considerable success, to increase their influence through the existing Labor Party. The influx of New Left elements has led the Labor Party to pursue a far more militant and anti-accommodational stance and has persuaded conservative party leaders to break away and establish their own party, the Democratic Socialists '70.

In sum, the changes have had the following impact on Dutch politics:

(1) There has been a sharp decline in the electoral following of the Catholic Party. (2) The electoral success of numerous splinter parties has cut into the near monopoly hitherto enjoyed by the bloc parties at the polls. (3) The Socialist party has become ideologically more militant.

THE EVOLUTION OF THE DECISION-MAKING PATTERN: THE END OF ACCOMMODATION?

Through the mid-1960s, the Dutch adhered closely to consociational decision-making. Ignoring Riker's minimum winning coalition maxim, they normally opted for great coalitions: in 16 of the 22 years from 1945 to 1967, four of the five bloc parties were partners in governing coalitions. During the 1950s, the heyday of consociational decision-making, the coalition parties normally controlled at least 75 percent of the parliamentary seats. As the largest party, at the ideological center, the Catholic Party has played a pivotal role in coalition politics, being a member of every postwar government. During most of the 1950s it joined forces with the Socialists and one or both of the Protestant parties; while during the 1960s, except for one brief interlude, the coalitions moved to the right with the Liberals replacing the Socialists. The conventional distinction between government and opposition parties, however, did not hold in the Netherlands. In this connection, Daalder (1966:221) writes:

> Even when a particular party has not been in the government, this has not prevented its allied subcultural interest groups from being closely involved in the making of government policy; second, although a party may have been outside the government, this has not necessarily induced it to engage in hard opposition tactics against the government; and, conversely, when a party has been a member of a government coalition, this has not necessarily implied warm support.

In addition, by adhering to such rules as the depoliticization of sensitive issues and the proportional allocation of scarce resources among the subcultures, Lijphart (1975) has argued, the Dutch political leaders have further buttressed the politics of accommodation. Basically, then, the bloc political leaders governed the Netherlands smoothly and efficiently and, at the same time, scrupulously avoided open conflict.

Yet over the past decade, accommodation politics have had trying times. The shrinking support for the confessional parties combined with the anti-accommodationist position of the Labor Party has made coalition formation a more arduous and drawn out process. And the cabinets eventually formed, Lijphart (1975) has observed, have become more short-lived. Furthermore, prior to the 1971 elections, the Socialists joined two progressive splinter parties to form an opposition group and a shadow cabinet. The opposition parties, as De Swaan (1973) points out, claimed that they would join any subsequent cabinet either together or not at all. For the first time in postwar Dutch politics, the Parliament was split between more or less conventional government and oppostion parties. More intangibly, the tone of ideological and partisan discussions has become more strident, not only among activists, but among elites as well. Van den Berg and Molleman (1974) see the rise of a new generation of leaders who will be less conciliatory than the great accommodators of the fifties and early sixties. Indeed, Den Uyl, the current prime minister, may be the last of the powerful accommodators. The new leaders, Van den Berg and Molleman predict, will be more reluctant to abandon clearly articulated partisan interests for the sake of accommodation.

These changes are rooted in the evolution of subcultural politics.

(1) The opposition of the new antiregime splinter parties, no matter how vague in its inspiration, has made the pragmatic-technocratic style of decision-making less acceptable.

(2) The traditional constraints on open competition designed to preserve harmony among the confessional subcultures have become increasingly superfluous as the religious issues have gradually receded from the Dutch political consciousness.

(3) By no means least, the very fluidity of partisan choices that has surfaced over the past decade has encouraged elite competition.

Occurring simultaneously, the processes of depillarization and polarization have exposed the enormous confessional electorates as a rich reservoir for the non-confessional, class parties. All this has produced a more lively, competitive political game.

Theoretical Interpretations

In the Netherlands there was, until the mid-1960s, an association between consociational decision-making and low levels of subcultural hostility. But as was the case for Switzerland and Austria, there is another plausible explanation for this low hostility; namely that in the two decades following World War II perceived deprivation among the subcultures was not pronounced. No subculture was compelled to resort to violence in order to alleviate or escape subordination. The crucial point is that subcultural segmentation is not synonymous with subcultural hostility. That the Dutch have continued to prefer to associate with members of their own subculture may reflect thorough socialization and segregation rather than deeply-rooted antagonisms. And while it is true that relations among members of different subcultures have usually been cool and distant, they also have been nearly always correct, courteous, and civil.

By the late forties the subcultures had realized their emancipation. Due perhaps to the results of earlier efforts at elite accommodation, the subcultures had achieved the goals—state support for religious schools, universal suffrage, and a comprehensive social welfare program—that originally had spurred the organization of the blocs. Yet the pillars lingered, perhaps because the bloc leaders wanted them to. The leaders realized that their authority rested on the willingness of the Dutch citizens to remain loyal to their respective subcultures. This was especially true for the leaders of the confessional blocs; given the integration of the disparate religious groups into a more homogeneous society, there was no longer a pressing need for multiple Catholic and Protestant social organizations. But the very competition among bloc leaders for readers, audiences, members, and voters may have perpetuated the pillarization which, Lijphart (1969) argues, would have threatened the viability of the system if not for the willingness of these same bloc leaders to accommodate at the elite level. Hence the bloc leaders may have been protecting the people against the segmentation they were sustaining.

In fact, the reluctance of bloc leaders to abandon the consociational pattern may have exacerbated relations between certain segments of Dutch society (Stiefbold, as we have seen, has made a similar argument for Austria). For example, trade union leaders, by failing to recognize that their followers' interests were not necessarily congruent with those espoused by management and government, and by accepting—presumably for the sake of sustained economic growth—one modest wage increment after another, may have unnecessarily soured rank-and-file union members who felt entitled to a more generous share of Dutch prosperity.

Since the mid-1960s Dutch politics have become more unstable as indicated by the increasing prevalence of civil disobedience, greater cabinet instability, and the strikes of non-unionized construction workers. Lijphart (1975) is puzzled by this greater instability. He contends that a consociational regime becomes depoliticized if elite cooperation is maintained in the face of declining subcultural segmentation, and that a depoliticized regime permits policy differences to be resolved through orderly, pragmatic negotiations among interested parties. But the recent evolution of Dutch politics fails to confirm this notion: in fact, as Dutch society has become *more* integrated, he contends, the Netherlands has become *less* instead of more stable. For Lijphart this is the second paradox of Dutch politics.

We do not consider this a paradox because we do not accept the premise that severe social conflict is alien to culturally homogeneous societies. Even with the demise of subcultural segmentation complex, industrial societies still face unresolved issues which may provoke hostilities. As a homogeneous society, the Netherlands, like such other homogeneous societies as England or Sweden, is still marked by relatively wide disparities in the allocation of wealth and authority. Though perhaps not organized along bloc lines, there are subordinate and dominant groups in these non-pillarized societies. The extent to which the subordinate group accepts the prevailing pattern of inequality and supports the status quo depends on complex sets of factors which are not considered by the consociational theory since it assumes that homogeneous societies, capable of coping with policy differences through peaceful bargaining, will be stable. If one considers the polarization of Dutch politics along class lines and the concomitant radicalization of the Socialist Party, the second Dutch paradox disappears: that heightened social conflict has strained the stability of the Dutch political system is no paradox.

5. BELGIUM

SUBCULTURAL CONFLICT AND
AD HOC CONSOCIATIONALISM

Since neither Switzerland, Austria, nor the Netherlands has been plagued by severe subcultural conflict since the late 1940s, it has been difficult to assess whether elite conciliation has actually contributed to or has been merely a symptom of social harmony. But in Belgium we finally come to a system which, in fact, has been troubled by vigorous subcultural conflict during the postwar era: hostilities between Catholics and anticlericals dominated Belgian politics for much of the 1950s while the regional/linguistic dispute between French- and Dutch-speakers has been politically salient since the early 1960s. As Zolberg (1974) demonstrates, both conflicts have deep historical roots and were the source of trouble in Belgium in earlier times. One might expect that the Belgian case would offer an excellent opportunity to determine whether and how consociational decision-making can successfully regulate subcultural conflict. Unfortunately, this is not so because, in contrast to the systems already discussed, Belgium has never managed to establish a stable, institutionalized form of elite accommodation. Since consociationalism in Belgium has been practiced on a more sporadic and ad hoc basis, and since it has been more "contaminated" by intense elite competition, it is relatively difficult to test conclusively Lijphart's principal hypothesis on the basis of the Belgian experience.

THE EVOLUTION OF THE
RELIGIOUS AND LANGUAGE CLEAVAGES

Although nearly all Belgians are Catholic—approximately 95 percent are baptized—less than half the population regularly attends church. Among nonpracticing Catholics, there has been—and to a lesser degree continues to be—a core of free-thinkers and anticlericals who have tried to minimize the influence of the Church in secular, and especially educational, affairs. While this division cuts across class and language cleavages, practicing Catholics are proportionately more numerous and the Church is more influential in Dutch-speaking Flanders than in French-speaking Wallonia. Based on the accounts offered by Lorwin (1971), and Dobbelaere (1966), Belgium resembles the Netherlands in the degree of pillarization along the confessional dimension (with the Calvinist pillar, of course, being absent in Belgium). Until the early 1960s, as indicated by Urwin (1970), the traditional Belgian parties accurately mirrored the religious division, with the Catholic party pitted against the anticlerical Socialists and Liberals.[15]

There is thus ample evidence to document the thorough social isolation of the Catholic, Socialist, and Liberal subcultures. The commonly accepted impression that, at least until the 1960s, there was considerable psychological hostility between Catholics and anticlericals, however, has not been tested by systematic empirical investigations. Yet there have been indications of conflict; and, as is so often the case, education has been the most contentious issue. The most recent major conflict, the so-called Second School War (1954-1958),[16] centered around the reduction of state support for Catholic secondary schools, and was terminated, at least temporarily, by the famous 1958 *pacte scolaire.*

Though minor skirmishes over the school question continued (especially among elites), the *pacte scolaire* depoliticized the religious issue. Ostensibly satisfied with the compromise embodied in the *pacte,* Belgians were not preoccupied with the religious dispute. When asked, in two separate surveys conducted during the mid-1960s, one by Huyse (1969) and the other by Delruelle et al. (1966), what were the most important problems facing Belgium, respondents did not cite state aid to Church schools or any other issue that could be linked directly to the religious cleavage (unfortunately, there are no comparable survey data for the 1950s). Furthermore, the temporary resolution of the school issue as well as the growing prominence of the linguistic conflict, which strained relations between Flemish and Francophone Catholics, cut sharply into the Catholic party's electoral support.[17] Based on 1968 survey data analyzed by Delruelle et al. (1970), it appears that this loss of support is due, in part, to the fact that younger voters (under 40), many of whom entered the electorate after the termination of the Second School War, have shifted their support from the Catholic and Socialist parties to the linguistic parties.

Despite this temporary depoliticization of the school issue after 1958, there are several indications that the confessional subcultures have persisted.

(1) Religious orientation still molds partisan choice for a large number of Belgian voters. In their 1968 survey, Delruelle et al. (1970) found that 87 percent of Catholic Party supporters but only 24 percent of Socialist supporters are practicing Catholics.

(2) Catholic schools, the chief socializing agency outside the family, have continued to prosper. In his 1967 survey study of educational preferences among Belgian parents, Deprez (1972) found that 88.5 percent of those parents who were religiously active and who had had a Catholic education sent their children to Catholic schools, compared to only 13.5 percent of those parents who were religiously inactive and who had been educated in public school. Given this link between religious orientation and socialization, on the one hand, and educational preferences on the other, it is not surprising that between 1958 and 1969—a period in which the Catholic party was losing considerable support—the percentage of Belgian children attending Catholic primary schools actually increased slightly.[18]

(3) In the most recent legislative elections (1974), the Catholic party increased its share of the vote from 29.7 percent in 1971 to 31.8 percent. True, this is a marginal gain; but it reversed a trend, as it was the first time since 1958 that the Catholics had not lost ground in legislative elections. This reversal may be linked to the revival of religious disputes over, on this occasion, the revision of the *pacte scolaire* and the relaxation of the abortion laws.[19] While these disputes have not fostered the level of hostilities associated with the Second School War of the 1950s, they do suggest that the religious cleavage, though politically dormant for more than a decade, is still politically relevant.

As of the early 1960s, language differences became the chief source of political conflict. These differences as described by Lorwin (1970) and Van den Brande (1967) cut across religious and class divisions; though, as we have already mentioned, proportionately more Flemings are practicing

Catholics and, as discussed by De Bie (1965), the Belgian upper class traditionally has spoken French rather than Dutch. The linguistic subcultures are not highly institutionalized. Urwin (1970) and Dunn (1972) stress the failure of the Belgian party system to institutionalize the linguistic conflict. There are no Flemish or Walloon pillars: Flemings and Walloons belong to the same parties, trade unions, insurance societies, which reflect religious and/or class rather than linguistic cleavages. While the social isolation commonly associated with pillarization is absent, linguistic communities, with a few notable exceptions, are territorially separated, and, consequently, contact across linguistic lines is limited.[20] Linguistic subculture identification is relatively pronounced though community solidarity and consciousness are more evident among Flemings. Symbols of this strong Flemish solidarity include Flemish holidays, flags, and anthems. In his survey study of 500 Walloon and Flemish secondary and university students, Servais (1970) has documented this variance in subcultural identity. He found that Flemish students responded more positively along four dimensions (good/bad; strong/weak; active/inactive; and organized/disorganized) to the term *moi comme Flamand* than to *moi comme Belge*. Walloon students were more ambivalent; they viewed *moi comme Wallon* as good but weak and disorganized, and to *moi comme Belge* they responded positively on all the dimensions except power. Servais accounts for the Walloons' positive orientation to their Belgian identification by reference to the traditional Francophone dominance of Belgian national life. Linguistic divisions have fostered extensive political and social conflict, linked to the multiple subordinate-dominant relations among the linguistic communities. On the one hand, the differential postwar economic development of the regions —as discussed by Meynaud et al. (1965), Huyse (1970), Lorwin (1970), Lefèvre (1972), Stephenson (1972), and Frognier et al. (1974)—has led Walloons, who have been mired in an extended postwar recession, to feel subordinate to the Flemings, who have experienced rapid economic expansion and prosperity.[21]

On their side, the Flemish leaders, eager to end the generations of Flemish cultural and social subordination and to abet the development of a Flemish community sentiment, have demanded greater cultural autonomy and the expulsion of the last pockets of Francophone influence in Flanders. Flemish grievances are described by Lorwin (1970), Claes (1973), Telemachus (1963), and Herremans and Coppieters (1967).

The most intractable linguistic conflict stems from Flemish opposition to the Francophone dominance in Brussels-capital. More precisely, as outlined by Claes (1968), Goriely (1971), and Herremans (1968),

Flemings have tried to halt the assimilation of the Flemish minority into the hegemonic Brussels Francophone culture and to stop the Francofication of the once predominantly Flemish suburbs surrounding the capital.

Complicating the conflict is the dispute, detailed by Van Wauve (1971) and Vanderburcht (1964), over extremists on both sides advocating a federal solution, with moderates espousing various degrees and forms of decentralization.

In response to heightened conflict, linguistic-regional parties have surfaced, and have won more than 20 percent of the vote in the last two legislative elections, to challenge the traditional parties.[22] Furthermore, there are definite signs of subcultural enmity. According to Servais (1970), Flemish and Walloon students responded negatively to the rival subculture along the good/bad dimension. Yet in a survey conducted during the 1960s by the Belgian society of Economics and Applied Mathematics (1967), more than 80 percent of the respondents believed that contact between Flemish and Francophone students should be encouraged. It should also be noted that while Belgian linguistic hostility appears quite significant in contrast to the calm in Switzerland, it pales in comparison to subcultural conflict in such other divided societies as Northern Ireland, the United States, and Cyprus. Though systematic data are unavailable, few deaths or injuries have resulted from linguistically inspired marches, demonstrations, or riots.[23]

ELITE RESPONSES TO
RELIGIOUS AND LINGUISTIC CONFLICTS

The reactions of Belgian political leaders to conflicts arising from the religious and linguistic cleavages suggest two difficulties with the consociational theory. First, political leaders, rather than transcending subcultural differences to avert mass unrest, may settle conflicts which they had originally precipitated. This is seen most clearly in the evolution of the Second School War during the 1950s. While we agree with Dunn (1972:13) that the school issue was resolved "in true consociational style by means of a *pacte scolaire* among the three parties, negotiated by a series of 'round table' conferences, and approved by the respective central committees in November 1958," we are troubled by his failure to stress that in formulating this *pacte,* the party leaders were settling a dispute which they themselves had initiated and prolonged. Following the 1950 elections, according to the account offered by Meynaud et al. (1965), leaders of the Catholic party, controlling a parliamentary majority for the first time since the First World War, unilaterally increased state subsidies to Catholic secondary schools without providing the funds necessary for the construction of an adequate number of additional public schools. In the absence of visible and intense public pressure, the Catholics, implementing tenets of their campaign platform, imposed their position on the opposition. And when the anticlerical Socialist-Liberal coalition was formed after the 1954 elections, the Catholic decision to raise the subsidies was reversed. The compromise settlement, which provided funds for public and Catholic schools and which was binding for 12 years, came only after an extended period of competitive majoritarian decision-making practices.

The Belgian experience tends to confirm the basic consociational hypothesis: competitive elite interaction extended and exacerbated religious subcultural conflict, while elite accommodation depoliticized the issue and reduced hostilities. On a more general level, however, the Belgian case does not support the consociational bias in favor of elite predominance. Typically, the students of the consociational theory argue that moderate bloc leaders preserve stability, despite the subculturally divided masses who, if not socially or physically isolated and placated by elite conciliation, would invariably be on the verge of violent confrontation. If this image were appropriate for Belgium, one would have expected elite hostility over the school issue to trigger mass disorder and violence. Instead, public violence was quite limited, despite efforts on the part of bloc leaders to mobilize their followers in extrasystemic protests.

Second, there are basic conceptual ambiguities in the model concerning what constitutes consociational decision-making. Thus observers disagree over exactly how the Belgian elites have reacted to the linguistic conflict: Dunn (1972) points to the erosion of elite accommodation since the early 1960s while Eric Nordlinger (1972) stresses how through cooperation the elites have played a positive role in regulating the conflict. That Dunn and Nordlinger offer these conflicting views is due, we would argue, to the conceptual confusion of the model. Depending on what criteria one applies, elite relations during the linguistic crisis could be categorized as conciliatory or competitive, as conforming to or departing from the consociational decision-making.

If consociationalism requires orderly negotiations among bloc leaders who preside over cohesive subcultures and who can command the support of the overwhelming majority of the members of their respective subcultures, then Belgium falls far short of the mark. With regard to the linguistic question, as Lorwin (1972), Dunn (1972), Urwin (1970), Huyse (1970), Ladrière (1970), Heisler (1974), and numerous others have demonstrated, the institutional infrastructure of consociationalism has not been present in Belgium. The political leadership of the communities has been fragmented; basically, four parties (the three traditional parties and one linguistic party) have represented the interests of each region. Each presenting a different conception of and solution to the problem, no party, no set of leaders can claim to speak for even a majority of Flemings, Walloons, or Bruxellois.

If consociationalism requires consensus among elites over compromise solutions, Belgium, once again, deviates from the model. As described by Grootaers (1971), Wigny (1972), Tindemans (1973), and De Stexhe (1972), the negotiations that preceded the passage of various linguistic reforms were chaotic, acerbic, and marked by frequent interruptions resulting from the withdrawal of one group or another from the proceedings.

If consociationalism requires elite initiatives that depoliticize the issues that divide the subcultures, Belgium again fails to adhere to the prescribed pattern. Meynaud et al. (1965) discuss how linguistic laws enacted in 1962 and 1963, contrary to elite intentions, further politicized rather than depoliticized the linguistic dispute. The laws infuriated many Francophones, especially those in Brussels-capital, without entirely satisfying the Flemings. In surveys conducted following the enactment of these laws by Huyse (1969) and Delruelle et al. (1970), it was demonstrated that Belgians were quite preoccupied with the linguistic question.

It would be inaccurate to adduce from these difficulties that the Belgian elite has pursued a competitive strategy. Indeed, several aspects of elite interactions since the early 1960s suggest the presence of a conciliatory spirit; a spirit in keeping with the consociational systems has been faithfully implemented, and, in fact, has been recently incorporated into the formal constitutional structure. Second, the Belgian Parliament has established numerous extra-parliamentary committees, which have also observed the proportionality principle in recruiting their members, that have served as forums where all sides are able to air their grievances and to articulate their demands free of the pressure and publicity typically attending parliamentary proceedings.

Third, and most important, Wigny (1972), De Stexhe (1972), Dunn (1974), and Heisler (1974) describe the elaborate and intricate set of constitutional reforms, aimed at settling the dispute, that were, in fact, adopted. While not always greeted with unanimous approval, these reforms did address the subcultures' major grievances. And this was remarkable, for, as Lorwin has perceptively noted, the dispute, which assumed a zero-sum character, did not lend itself to easy compromise solutions.[24] To end the imbroglio, political leaders made complex mutual adjustments on several issues: for instance, the rights granted the Francophone minority at the national level were also accorded the Flemish minority in Brussels-capital.

The elite response to the linguistic crisis suggests that even in segmented societies elite accommodation, though ad hoc and occasionally strained, can take place beyond the institutional confines stipulated by the consociational theory. Pillarization, bloc cohesion, and centralized bloc authority are not necessary conditions for a certain level of elite accommodation. In Belgium, the *pacte scolaire* was formulated by classical consociational methods while the 1970 constitutional reforms were reached through more ad hoc procedures.[25]

Perhaps this ad hoc consociationalism can explain why linguistic conflict in Belgium has been relatively moderate; demonstrations and riots have been spaced between long periods of public calm, and they have been relatively nonviolent when they have occurred. Nordlinger (1972) endorses this view. But this position fails to account for the remarkable patience of the Belgian people who shunned extreme violence while the political elites intermittently groped for nearly a decade toward a settlement. As illustrated by the 1974 Protestant strikes in Northern Ireland, the most genuine and ingenious attempts at elite conciliation can be sabotaged by mass recalcitrance.

6. CONCLUSIONS

Though our review of the literature does not reject the consociational theory, it does suggest several reservations.

First, the omnipotent, positive role it attributes to elites may be exaggerated and too simplistic. Since in most cases it is not demonstrated, but only inferred that subcultural segmentation is a potential cause of subcultural hostility, it is often difficult to determine if elite accommodation is a consequence or a cause of inter-subcultural calm. Moreover, when subcultural hostility is evident and relatively intense—as over the Jura problem and the Belgian linguistic dispute—elite accommodation has been difficult to achieve; and to the extent that it has been realized, has not been an especially successful conflict-regulating mechanism. Under the present conditions in Northern Ireland, for example, any plan for "power-sharing" could not possibly be implemented. More generally, given high levels of subcultural hostilities, elite accommodation may be irrelevant. In addition, elites may have abetted the persistence of the segmentation that, allegedly, would endanger the systems' stability if not for elite accommodation. In Belgium the bloc leaders are applauded for resolving a subcultural dispute for which they were largely responsible. Thus, the consociational image of pragmatic bloc leaders keeping the peace while potentially hostile subcultures are kept isolated fails to do justice to the complexities of the four systems we have analyzed.

Second, advocates of the consociational theory not only exaggerate the part played by elites in resolving conflict, they also neglect the importance of relative deprivation as a source of subcultural hostility. The degree to which scarce resources are, or are perceived to be, allocated inequitably among subcultures may be more significant than the degree of elite accommodation in explaining variations in the level of hostilities. Accordingly, we believe that the different levels of conflict in Belgium and Switzerland cannot be attributed primarily to differences in elite relations. That the Bernese have found it so difficult to resolve the Jura problem suggests that if the linguistic conflict should involve the subcultures at the national level, as has been the case in Belgium, Swiss leaders would face difficult problems similar to those which have troubled their Belgian counterparts. Lorwin (1972) stresses the inequality between Belgian language groups as a source of conflict:

> The Flemish still saw themselves as oppressed, despite the political weight of their numbers, the enhanced status of the Dutch language, and the economic modernization of Flanders. Michael Balfour's "reflexes of underdogs" continue far beyond the conditions that created them.

> So did the reflexes of "overdogs." The Walloons looked backward too, but to contrast past security with current decline and worse fears for the future.

Relations between the Swiss linguistic communities have not been marked by the sense of deprivation, prejudice, and insecurity that have fed the linguistic conflict in Belgium.

Third, contrary to the consociational position, a decline in segmentation along with continued elite consensus does not preclude severe social and political conflict. Persistent inequalities and deprivation in so-called homogeneous, nonsegmented societies may engender chronic social tensions. To the disadvantaged, continued elite consensus, justified as a means to preserve stability, may appear as a device to perpetuate the existing stratification system. The growing instability in the Netherlands despite the declining confessional segmentation and the gradual depillarization along the class dimension lends credence to this position.

In the light of these criticisms, can the theory be salvaged? Yes, but only in a far more modest form. If subcultural hostility is relatively moderate, consociational decision-making may further reduce hostility, which may in turn further strengthen consociationalism. Thus, a feedback process between decreasing hostility and expanding consociational decision-making patterns may develop. This feedback process may break down in the long run. Critics in the four countries have complained that elite consensus has ossified privileges and inequalities and has reduced the political role of the citizen. This may foster frustrations, and ultimately, even lead to the outbreak of violence. To prevent such a development, after a certain time consociational decision-making should give way to a more competitive mode. A decrease in the intensity of subcultural segmentation, which will probably result from consociational decision-making, should facilitate such a change; Austria has apparently made this shift. The cases of Switzerland and the Netherlands, however, suggest that the transition may be difficult.

In Switzerland, two of the political conditions which facilitated the shift in Austria are not present. For one thing, the Austrian parties are far more centralized and disciplined than the Swiss parties. Without this kind of centralization and discipline, governing parties which enjoy only a small parliamentary majority could not sustain stable cabinets. Furthermore, Austrian politicians need not concern themselves with a well-developed referendum system; in Switzerland, referenda could be used by opposition parties to block the smooth functioning of the government in power.

The Netherlands, like Austria, has changed in the mid-1960s from a consociational to a more competitive system. But contrary to Austria, the change has been associated with a rise in cabinet instability and increasing elite hostility. Why have the Austrians been able to make the transition more successfully? We would suggest:

First, the reduced prominence of religious issues did not have an unsettling impact on Austrian party politics because the Catholic party was able to assume a position on the left-right socioeconomic continuum as the spokesman for middle-class and conservative rural interests. The socially heterogeneous Dutch confessional parties, on the other hand, frustrated the expression of socioeconomic interests just when those interests were coming to dominate Dutch politics.

Second, the Austrians may be more sensitive than the Dutch to the potentially debilitating effects of open partisan conflict. The traumatic memories of the First Republic may serve to remind Austrians how subcultural conflict and a precarious national identity can cripple democratic politics. Since the Dutch, who have been practicing consociational decision-making since 1917, have never witnessed internal violence comparable to the Austrian Catholic-Socialist confrontations of the thirties, most Dutch leaders do not fear that a return to a more competitive pattern of political life would mean an outbreak of mass violence.

Third, drawing on the well-worn notion that external threats often sustain domestic political cohesion, it is plausible that Austria's relatively vulnerable position in the international system may also abet internal solidarity. As a neutral nation, not integrated into the Western defense system, bordering on the Soviet bloc and having been occupied by the Soviet Union for a decade following the Second World War, Austria, more than most other Western European nations, is sensitive to dissension within the communist bloc as well as between the superpowers. The Netherlands does not suffer from the same sense of insecurity.

Fourth, despite its postwar economic boom, Austria is still one of the less affluent of the Western democracies, and certainly less affluent than the Netherlands. One might speculate that, far more than the Dutch, the Austrians are still preoccupied with acquisitive, materialistic goals (Inglehart, 1971) and, therefore, are less inclined to challenge the established bourgeois value system.

Overall, we are not very optimistic about the long-range consequences of consociational decision-making. We would put our conclusions at least in more moderate tones than Lijphart (1975:vi) who claims that the politics of accommodation "is a normative model that is more appropriate than the pluralistic model for the world's many highly divided societies aspiring to democratic rule." We are aware, however, that the competitive model, too, faces severe difficulties, even in countries like Great Britain. Thus, consociational decision-making may in many cases be the lesser of two evils.

7. PROSPECTS FOR FURTHER RESEARCH

Despite its shortcomings, the consociational theory has a great potential if further developed. Its main strength, in our view, is its emphasis of elite decision-making as an explanatory variable. In the past, efforts to explain variations in violence have tended to neglect the mode of decision-making, treating it often as a "black box." Heavy emphasis has been given to variables of the environment such as economic development, urbanization, education, and relative deprivation. Almond has been one of the main spokesmen of this orientation. It is interesting that in a recent publication, Almond recognizes the need to explore the "black box" of political decision-making. He is certainly an unprejudiced witness since he has stressed in his earlier writings the importance of environmental factors. In this publication, Almond and eight collaborators studied seven historical crisis situations—for example Germany after World War I and the Meiji Restoration in Japan (Almond et al., 1973). The book concludes that macro-variables of the environment constrain the options of the politicians but leave the outcome undetermined. Almond et al. (1973:648-649) argue that

> Human choice, bargaining, risk-taking, skill, and chance must be considered to explain the actual outcome ... for political *science* this may be a disappointing conclusion, but for political problem solving there may be cause for satisfaction ... for if choices in politics are constrained but indeterminate, then the contemporary "doom" literature, based as it is on projections of macro-trends of population, technology, pollution, ever-widening gaps between the rich and the poor, etc. needs to be supplemented by a *political* science literature that stresses room for maneuver, ranges of freedom, the place for risk-taking.

Almond et al. (1973:647) want "to win back a bit of the autonomy of the political sphere, rehabilitate the role of human choice and creativity in developmental problem solving." However, this book does not present a political decision-making theory; Almond et al. (1973:621) state that they have "placed this issue on [their] agenda for future research and make no claims of having done anything more than to specify ways in which one could handle the leadership variable in such a way as to link it systematically with the other ... approaches to developmental causation." They encourage the readers "to share in this exploratory process."

The consociational theory is a good beginning in this direction in the sense that it treats the mode of political decision-making as a key theoretical variable. Political science, of course, has been always interested in modes of decision-making. Most studies, however, were atheoretical in their orientation. This holds particularly for many case studies about individual decisions; usually, they describe in great detail the way in which the decision is reached, but make no effort to classify the discovered form of decision-making in a broader typology; without such a typology all attempts at explanation remain at an ad hoc basis. Sometimes, the case studies are undertaken in a broader context, often to detect the power structure of a local community or a political party. But even such power studies are generally not really theoretical with regard to the mode of decision-making; the different modes are hardly ever systematically distinguished and explained in their causes and consequences.

The consociational theory has made a step forward in distinguishing two modes of decision-making and analyzing possible causes and consequences. This paper should have demonstrated, however, that the dichotomy of competitive and consociational decision-making is too simplistic and that a more exhaustive typology is needed. One of us is participating in a project (Steiner and Dorff, forthcoming), which attempts to develop a more subtle and comprehensive typology. The project deals with individual decisions as units of analysis. The context is the Free Democratic party of the canton Berne in Switzerland, which was studied by participant observation for 20 months. During this time, 111 meetings of various party committees were observed (executive committee, parliamentary group, and so on). In all these meetings, a total of 466 openly articulated disagreements were identified. The question was then, through what modes of decision-making were these conflicts resolved?

At first, the study seemed to strongly support the commonly accepted notion that Switzerland is, in a descriptive sense, a consociational democracy. Only 12 percent of the conflicts were regulated by the majority principle. Surprisingly, however, there were also relatively few cases that corresponded to consociationalism, defined as a situation in which all participants who have expressed an opinion finally agree on a common solution: this agreement may be expressed in a formal vote, orally, or just in a gesture. Thus, consociational decision-making does not necessitate the consent of all participants, but only of those who have expressed an opinion. Even applying this relatively broad definition, only 21 percent of all decisions could be classified as consociational.

What about the remaining 67 percent of the cases? It was relatively easy to classify 30 percent as non-decisions: at the end of the discussion no decision was taken at all. In one quarter of these cases the president of the meeting postponed the decision explicitly in his summary. Much more often, in three quarters of the cases, the discussion passed to the following agenda without any final action; thus, the decision was implicitly postponed. Should we consider nondecisions as consociational? There was an explicit, or at least an implicit, agreement that no decision should be taken. But this agreement was limited to a matter of procedure and not to the substance of the issue. The consociational literature is vague whether nondecisions should be considered as consociational. We would prefer to treat nondecisions as a special category.

Having dealt with decisions by majority rule, consociational decisions, and nondecisions, there were still 37 percent of the cases to be classified. At first, these remaining cases appeared to be a nonclassifiable residual category. But we believe now that we have found a category under which these cases can be subsumed in a meaningful way. We have coined the concept "decisions by interpretation." These decisions are characterized by the fact that one or a few of the participants interpret the essence of the decision, and that this interpretation can be made by the president of the meeting in his final summary or by the secretary in the minutes of the meeting. A decision by interpretation can also be taken in such a way that a few key actors interpret tacitly what the decision of the group is, and then direct the discussion so that the decision is implicitly taken.

No claim is made, of course, that the decision-making in the Free-Democratic Party of the canton Bern is representative of all Swiss parties, or even of Switzerland as a whole. The study nevertheless demonstrates the difficulties of classifying political decision-making as either majoritarian or consociational. We have already argued that it is difficult, if not impossible, to locate nondecisions on a continuum from majoritarian to consociational. The difficulties are even greater to locate decisions by interpretation on a continuum from majoritarian to consociational. One may be tempted to classify these decisions as tacit consociational, since no opposition is made when the essence of the discussion is interpreted. But the tacit acceptance of an interpretation does not necessarily mean the vanishing of the opposition. In the Free-Democratic party, it happened often in such situations that the opposition came up again in a later meeting. Are decisions by interpretation, then, tacit majoritarian decisions in the sense that the minority accepts its defeat without a formal vote? There are two objections to such a classification. First, it is often unclear who holds the numerical majority, since all participants rarely speak up. Second, the tacit acceptance of an interpretation may in many cases mean that the opposition has given up; but there may be reasons why the consent is not openly expressed.

It is our proposal to treat majoritarian decisions, consociational decisions, nondecisions, and decisions by interpretation as four different categories which cannot be located on a single continuum. These four categories can be used to classify not only individual decisions but the overall decision-making pattern of political systems. On this macro-level, one has to determine what mixture of decision-making modes a particular system has. A country could be characterized, for example, by a predominance of decisions by interpretation, a fair amount of non-decisions, and relatively few decisions by amicable agreement and majority votes. We recognize that such classifications are difficult but certainly not impossible. The most fruitful research strategy seems to analyze decision-making in a few key issue areas that can be compared cross-nationally, for example pollution control and the fight against inflation. One can then determine for different countries which decision modes are used more often than others.

A problem will be that in some countries certain issues will not appear on the political agenda. This is the problem discussed in the so-called nondecision literature (Bachrach and Baratz, 1962). We agree that this literature has made an important point, but we prefer a different terminology. We reserve the concept of nondecision for situations where an issue is put on the agenda but no decision is taken. This usage corresponds closely to everyday language; politicians and journalists usually speak of a nondecision only when an issue is formally debated but no decision is reached. If, on the other hand, an issue is not put on the agenda, they would hardly speak of a nondecision. We prefer here the concept of an *unexpressed conflict,* distinguishing three subcategories:

(1) Conflicts unexpressed in the process of agenda setting: the political decision-makers are aware of an issue but do not set it on their agenda.

(2) Conflicts unexpressed because of a lack of communication to the political decision-makers: some groups in the population are aware of an issue but this issue is not communicated to the political decision-makers.

(3) Conflicts unexpressed because of a lack of awareness in the population: a society has an underlying conflict but no one in this society is aware of this conflict, so that it does not develop into an issue.

Distinguishing between nondecisions and unexpressed conflicts and further differentiating within the latter concept, should help to clarify the confused debate that resulted from the work of Bachrach and Baratz (Wolfinger, 1971; Debnam, 1975). In classifying countries according to their decision-making modes, one should also take account of the extent to which conflicts are consciously or subconsciously not expressed. Analyzing unexpressed conflicts is, of course, not simple, but allowing for a certain softness in the data it is not impossible (Steiner and Dorff, forthcoming).

In summary, we propose as a first development of the consociational theory, to give up the simple dichotomy of consociational and competitive decision-making and to use a more exhaustive typology including also unexpressed conflicts. A second suggestion is to change the emphasis in theory-building from an inductive to a deductive method. Because it was primarily developed in an inductive way, the consociational theory oftentimes has a rather ad hoc character. Here, it is possible to learn from game theory in which the deductive method is applied in a rigorous way. Starting from basic axioms about the behavior of politicians, game theory has developed a coherent set of hypotheses (Riker and Ordeshook, 1973). The most fundamental axiom is that politicians only try ot maximize their individual power. We criticize elsewhere (Steiner and Dorff, forthcoming) that this axiom is too simple and that we should allow the possibility that other values, besides power, may be important for politicians. We propose as additional values prestige, group solidarity, rectitude, and free time. The weight of the individual values would not be constant, but would vary from actor to actor and for each actor from situation to situation. If in a particular situation the values are not compatible, the actors would try to optimize each value under the constraints of all other values.

(1) Power and prestige are closely related but not identical values. By power in a decision-making situation we mean the capacity of an actor to make other group members do things that they would not have done otherwise. (2) Prestige is the esteem and the respect that one gets from the other group members. Empirically, the two values are probably closely related: a powerful actor tends to have prestige, and a prestigious person tends to have power. Yet, the two values may not always go together; an actor who exercises a great deal of power may lose prestige, because he is perceived as too selfish. There are also sources other than power for prestige; an actor who helps to structure the discussion, procures valuable information, and clarifies the alternatives for the decision may get much prestige from his colleagues.

It is our assumption that both power and prestige may be maximized in a decision-making situation. This does not necessarily mean that each actor tries to maximize both values; some actors may be interested only in power, others only in prestige. It is also possible that one value is seen as an end in itself; the other value is simply a means to attain this end. If an actor is only interested in maximizing power, he may see prestige as an instrument to increase his power. Others may want to maximize prestige as an end in itself and use power only in instrumental terms.

(3) Group solidarity exists if the members of a group have a feeling of togetherness, a we-feeling, a sense of identity. For many actors, group solidarity is an end in itself; it may satisfy an emotional need to belong to a warm and closely-knit group of friends and colleagues. Other actors may use group solidarity in an instrumental way, for example to increase their power; perhaps a decision has been taken according to their wishes, but they anticipate that the decision can only be implemented if the solidarity of the group is strong enough.

(4) Rectitude is used in the sense of Lasswell (1958). An actor may be in a hopelessly losing position, but he insists in making his minority point, even if such a course of action decreases his power and prestige and

disrupts group solidarity. The motivation for such an action may be rectitude, the need to do the "right" thing, even if this hurts other values. In assuming rectitude as a key value, we are of course far from the assumptions of game theory. To assume such a value may seem "old-fashioned" and naive, but perhaps politicians act, at least sometimes, in an "old-fashioned" and naive way.

(5) The fifth value that we include is free time. We treat time as scarce resource. Nobody has endless time to participate in a particular decision-making situation. Most participants get uneasy after a certain duration of discussion; they begin to perceive a continuation of the discussion as a loss of time. They long for free time, so that they can move on to other decision-making situations; it may also be that they just want leisure time outside politics.

Having described the five values that we assume to be important in most decision-making situations, the question arises: why not add a sixth, a seventh, and so on. In observing the Free Democratic party in Switzerland, we learned about many more values that are supposedly important for the decision-making behavior. Various policy goals were particularly frequently mentioned. At formal meetings and informal gatherings, it was often said that a desire for clean water and other policy goals were the motivations for a particular behavior. We do not doubt that such policy goals may be important motivations, but we think we are able to take account of these goals with our five values. If an actor has a particular policy goal, he will most likely try to maximize power in order to win. In this case, power would not be an end in itself, but a means to attain the policy goal. The same actor may also try to maximize solidarity because he anticipates that a decision about his policy goal cannot be implemented without a high amount of group solidarity. The general value of rectitude is probably also important, whatever the particular substance of the policy goal may be. In this sense we try not to neglect policy goals, without being forced, however, to include a long list of individual goals.

Stating in an explicit way the values that we expect politicians to maximize should help to develop a theory which has a more deductive character than the existing consociational theory. The relative complexity of our behavioral axioms, however, will not allow as much mathematical elegance as in game theory. But we hope that we will get a closer fit with reality than is attained in game theory. We share the concern of Almond that "highly formalistic mathematical models" should not be ends in themselves and that going too far in this direction may "be counter-productive." As Almond et al., "we decided to adopt a freer and less formalistic approach to model building." (For our attempt to develop a theory in this direction, see Steiner and Dorff, forthcoming.)

Besides a more exhaustive decision-making typology and a stronger emphasis on deductive theory building, we propose to treat subcultural segmentation not as a parameter but as a variable of the theory. In the consociational theory, subcultural segmentation is taken as a parameter which delimits the applicability of the theory to segmented systems. Sometimes, it is a good research strategy to limit the applicability to narrowly defined conditions. In the case of the consociational theory, however, the limitation to subculturally segmented systems has caused major problems, because there is confusion about where the borderline between segmented and nonsegmented systems should be drawn. As we have seen in this paper, there is even a debate whether Switzerland, Austria, the Netherlands, and Belgium—the four "classical" consociational countries—are really subculturally segmented. In taking subcultural segmentation as a built-in variable, one could escape such debates; there would also be the advantage that the generality of the theory could be extended. The theory would now apply to all levels of subcultural segmentation, and the knowledge of this level could help to explain why in a particular country certain modes of decision-making are preferred over others. Besides the *level* of segmentation, the theory would also have to take account of the *kind* of segmentation, distinguishing, for example, between religiously and linguistically based segmentation (Barry, 1975). In this sense, it should be possible to develop the consociational theory into a broader decision-making theory.

NOTES

1. The question was: "Which of these terms *best* describes the way you usually think of yourself? Genevois (for example), Swiss Romand (for example), Swiss."

2. The Social Democrats were already represented in the Federal Council from 1943 to 1953 but not yet on a proportionate basis.

3. At present, the French-speaking minority is about 15 percent of the canton.

4. Until November 1971, the SPOe had a minority government.

5. "Bereichsopposition" can be translated as opposition politics restricted to certain issues, "Bereichskoalition" as coalition politics restricted to certain issues.

6. The Catholic, Socialist, and Liberal pillars are each represented by one party while two parties—the Anti-Revolutionary Party and the Christian Historical Union—represent Calvinist interests.

7. Thus between 1966 and 1970 there was a decline in Church attendance, the number of priests ordained, the percentage of Catholics christened. During the same period there was also an increase in resignations from the priesthood and mixed marriages solemnized in the Roman Catholic Church. See Thurlings (1971b).

8. Thurlings (1971a:132) describes the character of the difficulties in the following terms:

This crisis situation is attributable to an unavoidable side effect of newly-established open-mindedness, the corrosion of internal discipline. All aspects of the traditional ethic and doctrines became the subject of discussion. For the Catholic leaders the new situation meant nothing less than a status revolution within the Church whereby the administrative elite, whose role was the maintenance of discipline, saw their leadership threatened by the elite of theologians and other intellectuals, whose role was precisely such a critical study of their own Catholic culture, including its ethics and doctrines.

9. It should be noted, however, that many Dutch Catholic schools have discarded some of their "parochial, Catholic" characteristics; and, consequently, the differences between Catholic and public schools are not as great as they once were.

10. For the Catholic subculture the distance between religion and politics has always been larger than for the Calvinist structure. The KVP itself has always had a strong trend to integrate the party around a common program rather than around common (confessional or philosophical) principles. In its extreme form this trend has produced serious proposals to "deconfessionalize" the party. See Janse (1967-1968) and Couwenberg (1968-1969).

Although the process of deconfessionalization has been less severe for the Protestant bloc, Protestants, too, are now less inclined to vote on the basis of religious sentiments. In recent elections, the religiously doctrinaire Anti-Revolutionary Party and, especially, the more moderate Christian Historical Union have not been able to match their electoral successes of the 1940s and 1950s. In the five elections between 1946 and 1959, the major confessional parties together won an average of 50.6 percent of the vote; but in 1972 they captured only 31.7 percent of the vote.

11. There are:

- in 1959 the Pacifistisch Socialistische Partij, P.S.P. (the Pacifist Socialist Party).
- in 1963 the Boerenpartij, B.P. (the Farmers' Party).
- in 1967 the Democraten '66, D'66.
- in 1971 the Politieke Partij Radicalen, P.P.R. (the Political Party of the Radicals).
- also in 1971 the Democratische Socialisten '70, D.S. '70 (the Democratic Socialist Party).

Of these, the B.P. is a rightist party, with some Poujadist overtones, championing the cause of the farmers and the small independents, protesting against the pressures of the welfare state apparatus. The P.S.P. is essentially a left-wing secession from the Labor Party and the P.P.R. comes mainly from the left-wing of the K.V.P. On the other hand, D.S. '70 is a right wing offspring from the Labor Party.

12. In 1967, the D'66 won 4.5 percent of the vote and expanded its share of the vote to 6.8 percent in 1971 before losing ground to 4.2 percent in 1972. It fared even worse in the 1974 provincial elections. For discussions of the party and its program, see Godschalk (1969-1970), Jacobs and Jacobs-Wessels (1968-1969).

13. By permitting annual wage increments which would only match increases in the cost of living without increasing the workers' standard of living, the Dutch hoped to limit inflation and to free investment capital for industrial development. Leaders of the three major federations of trade unions accepted wage controls as the best means to stimulate the economic growth necessary to guarantee full employment for an expanding labor force. Despite rapid economic growth, sharp increases in

corporate profits, and scarcity of labor, rank-and-file union members were willing to go along with their leaders' acceptance of the modest wage increments granted by the government. Through the late 1960s, wildcat and sanctioned strikes were quite rare; among Western European democracies, only Sweden, West Germany, and Switzerland lost fewer work days through strikes. See Windmuller (1969:390).

14. Among those reasons cited by Peper (1973:12) for the deterioration in industrial relations are the accelerated postwar industrialization which created an

Industrial climate conducive to more militant unionism, a decline in deference among young workers who are unwilling to fall docilely in place behind their union leaders and a growing number of industrial mergers which have led to widespread dismissal of workers.

15. For a discussion of the role confessional interests play in pressure groups, see Claeys (1973).

16. The first School War took place between 1878 and 1884 and it was precipitated by Liberal efforts to limit the role of religious instruction in public primary schools. See Terlinden (1929).

17. The Catholics' share of the popular vote dropped from an average of 44.3 percent in the five legislative elections between 1946 and 1958 to an average of 33.9 percent for the five elections held since 1958.

18. As in the Netherlands, then, political deconfessionalization has not led to a sharp decline in Catholic school enrollments. The reason for this might be that while linguistic cross-pressures may encourage, say a Dutch-speaking Catholic to abandon the Catholic party in favor of the more militant Flemish nationalist party, they may not affect his choice regarding where to send his children to school. Since the available option, except in Brussels, is between a Dutch-language Catholic school and a Dutch-language public school, he can offer his children a Catholic education without compromising his loyalty to the Flemish subculture.

19. For an excellent summary of some of the key issues in the revision of the *pacte scolaire,* see Jean Delfosse (1972). The Autumn 1973 issue of *La Revue Nouvelle* is devoted to discussions of the abortion issue in general and, more particularly, in Belgium.

20. A linguistic frontier running from west to east separates Dutch-speaking Flanders to the north from French-speaking Wallonia to the south. Brussels-capital is a bilingual enclave in Flanders situated just north of the linguistic frontier. In Brussels-capital the absence of pillars has facilitated extensive mingling between Flemish and Francophone residents. See Boeynaems (1973) and Goriely (1971).

21. As a permanent minority in a highly centralized state, the Walloons have complained that their economic woes have been neglected by Brussels' financial interests and by an unsympathetic Flemish national majority. Accordingly, they have demanded greater economic decentralization to assure themselves control over the region's economic reconstruction.

22. The Volksunie is the Flemish nationalist party, the "Front Démocratique des Francophones" (FDF) represents "militant" Francophones in Brussels, and the "Rassemblement Wallon" (RW) represents "militant" interests in Wallonia.

23. See Taylor and Hudson (1972:88-116). These data do not distinguish the sources of violence; but even if we assume that all the violence reported was related to the linguistic dispute, linguistic conflict has been much less extensive than in Northern Ireland or the United States.

24. For example, French-language public facilities either were or were not provided to the Francophone minorities in the Brussels suburbs; no decision could satisfy both sides.

25. As in the other systems we reviewed, there have been criticisms concerning the quality of Belgian democracy. Thus, Huyse (1970) notes the tendency, common in Austria and the Netherlands, for political leaders to emphasize the ideological differences among the blocs when mobilizing support among their followers, but then to adopt a more pragmatic course in negotiations among themselves. That bloc alternatives fade in the process of elite accommodation, he argues, limits the citizen's opportunity to shape the political process. In his study of public opinion, he draws on survey data to document the paucity of political interest and information among Belgian women and workers. For Huyse, this apathy is a sign of the inadequate political integration of certain subordinate groups in Belgian society, and, as such, constitutes a potential source of social disorder. Dewachter (1967), like Huyse, is critical of Belgian democracy. He complains that because oligarchical procedures are used to select candidates and to elect legislators, political leaders are not sufficiently accountable to the public. But Debuyst (1967), describing the same selection mechanisms, is more ambivalent about the impact of the recruitment process on the quality of Belgian democracy.

REFERENCES

ALMOND, G. A., S. C. FLANAGAN, and R. J. MUNDT [eds.] (1973) Crisis, Choice and Change. Boston: Little, Brown.

Année Politique Suisse (1965-) Centre de recherche de politique suisse à l'Université de Berne.

BACHRACH, P. and M. S. BARATZ (1962) "Two faces of power." Amer. Pol. Sci. Rev. 56:947-952.

BARRY, B. (1975) "Political accommodation and consociational democracy," British J. of Pol. Sci. 5:477-505.

BLUHM, W. T. (1973) Building an Austrian Nation. The Political Integration of a Western State. New Haven and London: Yale Univ. Press.

BODZENTA, E. and N. FREYTAG (1972) "Soziale Ungleichheit," pp. 100-136 in E. Bodzenta (ed.) Die oesterreichische Gesellschaft. Vienna: Springer Verlag.

BOEYNAEMS, M. (1973) "La Belgique démographique et politique en chiffres." Res Publica 15:385-393.

CLAES, L. (1973) "Le mouvement flamand entre la politique, l'économique et le culturel." Res Publica 15:219-235.

––– (1968) "Point de vue flamand sur Bruxelles." La Revue Nouvelle 48:90-95.

CLAEYS, P. H. (1973) Groupes de pression en Belgique. Brussels: Editions de l'Université de Bruxelles–Editions du Centre de Recherche et d'Informations Socio-Politique.

COUWENBERG, S. W. (1968-1969) "Discussie rond K.V.P." Acta Politica 4:104-111.

DAALDER, H. (1974a) "The consociational democracy theme." World Politics 26:604-621.

––– (1974b) "The Dutch universities between the 'new democracy' and the 'new management.'" Minerva (London) 12:221-257.

——— (1971) "On building consociational nations: the cases of the Netherlands and Switzerland." Internatl. Soc. Sci. J. 23:355-370.

——— (1966) "The Netherlands: opposition in a segmented society," pp. 188-236 in R. A. Dahl (ed.) Political Opposition in Western Democracies. New Haven: Yale Univ. Press.

De BIE, P. (1965) "Aspects socio-culturels des classes sociales ascendantes en Belgique." Cahiers Internationaux de Sociologie 39:91-109.

DEBNAM, G. (1975) "Nondecisions and power: the two faces of Bachrach and Baratz." Amer. Pol. Sci. Rev. 69:889-899.

De BRUYN, L.P.J. (1972) "Verzuiling en politieke deconfessionalissering." Acta Politica 7:42-47.

DEBUYST (1967) La fonction parlementaire en Belgique: Mécanismes d'accès et images. Brussels: Centre de Recherche et d'Informations Socio-Politique.

DELFOSSE, J. (1972) "Pluralisme interne ou pluralism externe?" La Revue Nouvelle 56:118-133.

DELRUELLE, N., R. EVALENKO, and W. FRAEYS (1970) Le comportement politique des électeurs belges. Brussels: Editions de l'Institut de Sociologie. Université Libre de Bruxelles.

DELRUELLE, N., J. COENEN, and D. MAIGRAY (1966) "Les problèmes qui préoccupent les Belges." Revue de l'Institut de Sociologie 34:291-341.

DEPREZ, G. (1972) "Le choix d'une école catholique." Recherches Sociologiques: 3:92-100.

De STREXHE, P. (1972) La révision de la constitution Belge 1968-1971. Brussels: Ferdinand Larcier.

De SWAAN, B. (1973) "Parties, policies, and pivots: coalition politics in the Netherlands." Delta 16:65-80.

DEWACHTER, W. (1967). Dewetgevende verkiezingen als proces van machtsverwerving in het Belgisch politiek. Antwerp: Standaard Wetenschappelijke Uitgeverij.

DOBBELAERE, K. (1966) Sociologische analyse van de Katholiciteit. Antwerp: Standaard Wetenschappelijke Uitgeverij.

DUNN, J. A., Jr. (1974) "The revision of the constitution in Belgium: a study in the institutionalization of ethnic conflict." Western Pol. Q. 27:143-163.

——— (1972) "Consociational democracy and language conflict: a comparison of the Belgian and Swiss experiences." Comparative Pol. Studies 5:9-16.

ENGELMAN, F. C. and M. A. SCHWARTZ (1974a) "Austria's consistent voters." Amer. Behavioral Scientist 18:97-110.

——— (1974b) "Partisan stability and the continuity of a segmented society: the Austrian case." Amer. J. of Sociology 79:948-966.

FISCHER, H. (1973) "Empirisches zur Arbeit des Nationalrates in der XIII. Gesetzgebungsperiode." Oesterreichische Zeitzchrift fuer Politikwissenschaft. 2:77-94.

FORSTER, P., H. ZIMMERMAN, O. FREI, and K. MUELLER (1974) Schwierige Selbstbestimmung im Jura. Hintergruende eines Minderheitproblems. Zurich: Buchverlag Neue Zuercher Zeitung.

FROGNIER, A., V. E. McHALE, and D. PARANZINO (1974) Vote, clivages socio-politiques et développement régional en Belgique. Louvain: Vander.

GADOUREK, I. (1961) A Dutch Community: Social and Cultural St———— Process in a Bulb-Growing Region in the N————————. sec. ed. Groningen: Wolters.

GERLICH, P. (1972) "Politisches System und Integration," in E. Bodzenta (ed.) Die oesterreichische Gesellschaft. Vienna: Springer Verlag.

GERMANN, R. E. (1975) Politische Innovation und Verfassungsreform. Ein Beitrag zur schweizerischen Diskussion ueber die Totalrevision der Bundesverfassung. Berne and Stuttgart: Verlag Paul Haupt.

GILG, P. (1969) "Parteien und eidgenoessische Finanzpolitik." Schweizerisches Jahrbuch fuer Politische Wissenschaft, 9:41-74.

GLASS, H. E. (1975) "Subcultural segmentation and consensual politics: the Swiss experience." Ph.D. dis. Chapel Hill: Univ. of North Carolina.

GLASTRA VAN LOON, J. F. (1967-1968) "Demokratie in Nederland." Acta Politica 3:185-213.

GODSCHALK, J. J. (1969-1970) "Enige politieke en sociale kenmerken van de oprichters van D'66." Acta Politica 5:62-74.

GORIELY, G. (1971) "Rapport introductif sur Bruxelles et le fédéralisme." Res Publica 13:397-422.

GOUDSBLOM, J. (1967) Dutch Society. New York: Random House.

GROOTAERS, J. (1971) "La révision de la constitution (I): L'évolution des idées et des textes jusqu'en Juillet 1970." Courrier Hebdomadaire Crisp 518-519 (April 22).

GRUNER, E. (1969) Die Parteien in der Schweiz. Berne: Francke Verlag.

HEISLER, M. O. (1974) "Institutionalizing societal cleavages in a cooptive polity: the growing importance of the output side in Belgium." pp. 178-200 in M. O. Heisler (ed.) Politics in Europe. New York: David McKay.

HENECKA, H. P. (1972) Die jurassischen Separatisten. Eine Studie zur Soziologie des ethnischen Konflikts und der sozialen Bewegung. Meisenheim am Glan: Verlag Anton Hain.

HERREMANS, M. P. (1968) "Attitudes des mouvements Flamands at Wallons à l'égard de Bruxelles." Le Revue Nouvelle. 48:298-304.

HERREMANS, M. P. with the collaboration of F. COPPIETERS (1967) The Language Problem in Belgium. Brussels: Belgian Info. and Documentation Inst.

HOFFMANN-NOWOTNY, H. J. (1973) Soziologie des Fremdarbeiterproblems. Eine theoretische und empirische Analyse am Beispiel der Schweiz. Stuttgart: Enke.

HUGHES, C. (1962) The Parliament of Switzerland. London: Cassell.

HUYSE, L. (1970) Passiviteit, Pacificatie en Verzuiling in de Belgische Politiek. Antwerp: Standaard Wetenschappelijke Uitgeverij.

――― (1969) L'apathie politique. Antwerp and Brussels: Editions Scientifiques Eraseme.

IMBODEN, M. (1964) Helvetisches Malaise. Zurich: EVZ Verlag.

INGLEHART, R. and D. SIDJANSKI (1974) "Dimension gauche-droite chez les dirigeants et électeurs suisses." Revue Française de Science Politique 24:994-1025.

INGLEHART, R. (1971) "The silent revolution in Europe: intergenerational change in post-industrial societies." Amer. Pol. Sci. Rev. 65:991-1017.

JACOBS, A.A.J. and W. JACOBS-WESSELS (1968-1969) "Duidelijkheid in de Netherlands politiek," Acta Politica 4:41-54.

JANSE, C.S.L. (1967-1968) "Spanningen in de K.V.P." Acta Politica 3:269-285.

JENNY, B. A. (1966) Interessenpolitik und Demokratie in der Schweiz: Dargestellt am Beispiel der Emser Vorlage. Zurich: Polygraphischer Verlag.

KEECH, W. P. (1972) "Linguistic diversity and political conflict: some observations based on four Swiss cantons." Comparative Politics 4:387-404.

KERR, H. H., Jr. (1974) Switzerland: Social Cleavages and Partisan Conflict. Sage Professional Papers in Contemporary Political Sociology, 1, 06-002, London and Beverly Hills: Sage Pub.

KNEUCKER, R. F. (1973) "Austria: an administrative state. The role of Austrian bureaucracy." Oesterreichische Zeitschrift fuer Politikwissenschaft 2:95-127.

KOCHER, G. (1967) Verbandseinfluss auf die Gesetzgebung. Aerzteverbindung, Krankenkassenverbaende un die Teilrevision 1964 des Kranken-und Unfallversichungsgesetzes. Berne: Francke Verlag.

KRUIJT, J. P. (1959) Verzuiling. Zandijk Heynis.

KUYPERS, G. (1967) Het politieke spel in Nederland. Meppel: Boom.

LADRIERE, J. (1970) "Le système politique belge, situation 1970." Courrier Hebdomadaire Crisp 500 (November 20).

LASSWELL, H. (1958) Who Gets What, When, How. Cleveland and New York: World.

LEFEVRE, J. (1972) "Pour une sociologie des relations entre groups linguistiques: un modèle d'analyse." Recherches Sociologiques 3:44-81.

LEHMBRUCH, G. (1974) "A non-competitive pattern of conflict management in liberal democracies: the case of Switzerland, Austria, and Lebanon," pp. 90-97 in K. McRae (ed.) Consociational Democracy. Toronto: McClelland & Stewart.

——— (1971) "Das politische System Oesterreichs in vergleichender Perspektive." Oesterreichische Zeitschrift fuer oeffentliches Recht. 22:35-56.

——— (1967a) "A non-competitive pattern of conflict management in liberal democracies: the case of Switzerland, Austria, and Lebanon." Paper presented at Seventh World Congress of Internatl. Pol. Sci. Assn., Brussels; published in K. McRae [ed.] (1974) Consociational Democracy. Toronto: McClelland & Stewart.

——— (1967b) Proporzdemokratie. Politisches System und Politische Kultur in der Schweiz und in Oesterreich. Tuebingen: Mohr.

LIJPHART, A. (1975) The Politics of Accommodation: Pluralism and Democracy in the Netherlands, sec. ed. Berkeley: Univ. of California Press.

——— (1969) "Consociational democracy." World Politics 21:207-225.

——— (1967) "Typologies of democratic systems." Paper presented at Seventh World Congress of the Internatl. Pol. Sci. Assn., Brussels; an extended version was published (1969) as "Consociational democracy." World Politics 21:207-225.

LORWIN, V. R. (1972) "Linguistic pluralism and political tension in modern Belgium," pp. 386-412 in J. A. Fishman (ed.) Advances in the Sociology of Language, vol. II. Selected Studies and Applications. The Hague: Mouton.

——— (1971) "Segmented pluralism: ideological cleavages and political cohesion in the smaller European democracies." Comparative Politics 3:141-175.

——— (1970) "Linguistic pluralism and political tension in modern Belgium" Canadian J. of History 5:1-23.

MASON, H. (1974) "Reflections on the politicized university: II. triparty and tripolarity in the Netherlands." AAUP Bulletin 60:383-400.

MAYER, K. B. (1969) "Einige soziologische Aspekte des Jura Problems." Schweizerische Zeitschrift fuer Volkswirtschaft und Statistik 105:230-236.

McRAE, K. [ed.] (1974) Consociational Democracy. Political Accommodation in Segmented Societies. Toronto: McClelland & Stewart, Carleton Library No. 79.

MEYNAUD, J., J. LADRIERE, and F. PERIN (1965) La décision politique en Belgique: Le pouvoir et les groupes. Paris: Armand Colin.

NASSMACHER, K. (1968) Das oesterreichische Regierungssystem. Grosse Koalition oder alternierende Regierung? Cologne and Opladen: Westdeutscher Verlag.

NEIDHART, L. (1970) Plebiszit und pluralitaere Domokratie. Eine Analyse der Funktion des schweizerischen Gesetzesreferendums. Berne: Francke Verlag.

NOORDZIJ, G. P. (1972) "Veranderingen in opvattingen van kiezers sinds 1967." Acta Politica 7:19-29.

NORDLINGER, E. A. (1972) Conflict Regulation in Divided Societies. Cambridge: Occasional Papers in Internatl. Affairs No. 29, Harvard Univ. Press.

PELINKA, A. (1973) "Repraesentative und plebiszitaere Elemente im oesterreichischen Regierungssystem." Oesterreichische Zeitschrift fuer Politikwissenschaft 2:33-47.

PEPER, B. (1973) "Changes in progress: Dutch industrial relations today." Delta 16:5-9.

POWELL, G. B., Jr. (1970) Social Fragmentation and Political Hostility. An Austrian Case Study. Stanford: Stanford Univ. Press.

RAE, D. W. and M. TAYLOR (1970) The Analysis of Political Cleavages. New Haven and London: Yale Univ. Press.

RIKER, W. H. and P. C. ORDESHOOK (1973) An Introduction to Positive Political Theory. Englewood Cliffs: Prentice-Hall.

SERVAIS, P. (1970) "Le sentiment national en Flandres et en Wallonie: Approche psycholinguinstique." Recherches Sociologiques 1:123-144.

SIDJANSKI, D., C. ROIG, H. KERR, R. INGLEHART, and J. NICOLAS (1975) Les Suisses et la politique. Enquête sur les attitudes des électeurs suisses. Berne: Herbert Lang.

SIDJANSKI, D. (1974) "Interest groups in Switzerland." Annals of the Amer. Academy of Pol. and Soc. Science 413:101-123.

Société Belge d'économie et de mathematique appliquées (1967) L'opinion publique belge et l'Université de Louvain. Louvain: Accociation du corps académique et du personnel scientifique de l'Université de Louvain.

STEINER, J. (1974) Amicable Agreement Versus Majority Rule. Conflict Resolution in Switzerland. Chapel Hill: Univ. of North Carolina Press.

––– and R. DORFF (forthcoming) Modes of Political Decision-Making. A Theoretical View.

STEINER, K. (1972) Politics in Austria. Boston: Little, Brown.

STEPHENSON, G. V. (1972) "Cultural regionalism and the unitary state idea in Belgium." Geographical Review 62:501-523.

STIEFBOLD, R. P. (1974) "Segmented pluralism and consociational democracy in Austria: problems of political stability and change," in M. O. Heisler (ed.) Politics in Europe. New York: David McKay.

TAYLOR, C. E. and M. C. HUDSON (1972) World Handbook of Political and Social Indicators, sec. ed. New Haven and London: Yale Univ. Press.

TELEMACHUS [pseud.] (1963) "Approche sociologique de la question linguistique." La Revue Nouvelle 38:303-314.

TERLINDEN, C. (1929) Histoire politique interne: Formation et évolution des partis. Histoire de la Belgique Contemporaine 1830-1914, vol. 2. Brussels: Albert Dewit.

THURLINGS, J.M.G. (1971a) "The case of Dutch Catholicism: a contribution to the theory of the pluralistic society." Sociologica Neerlandica 7:118-136.

——— (1971b) De wankele zuil. Nederlandse Katholieken tussen assimilatie en pluralism. Nijmegen: Dekker en Van de Vegt.

TINDEMANS, L. (1973) Dagboek van de Werkgroep Eyskens. Lier: Van In.

URIO, P. (1972) L'affaire des Mirages. Décision administrative et contrôle parlementaire. Geneva: Editions médicine et hygiène.

URWIN, D. (1970) "Social cleavages and political parties in Belgium: problems of institutionalization." Political Studies 28:32-40.

VAN DEN BERG, J. Th. and H.A.A. MOLLEMAN (1974) Crisis in de Nederlandse Politiek. Alphen aan den Rijn: Samson.

VAN DEN BRANDE, A. (1967) "Elements for a sociological analysis of the impact of the main conflicts on Belgian political life." Res Publica 9:437-470.

VANDERBURCHT, D. (1964) Belgen op de tweesprong; tussen nationalism en federalism. Antwerpen: Europese Federalistische Beweging.

VAN KEMANADE, J. A. (1968) De kathiolieken en hun onderwijs. Meppel: Boom.

VAN WAUWE, L. (1971) Fédéralisme: Utopie ou possibilité. Paris: R. Pichon & R. Durand-Auzias.

VODOPIVEC, A. (1966). Die Balkanisierung Oesterreichs. Die grosse Koalition und ihr Ende. Vienna and Munich: Verlag Fritz Molden.

WEILENMANN, H. (1951) Pax Helvetica oder die Demokratie der kleinen Gruppen. Erlenbach and Zurich: Rentsch Verlag.

WELAN, M. (1975) "Vom Proporz zum Konkurrenzmodell: Wandlungen der Opposition in Oesterreich," pp. 151-176 in H. Oberreuter (ed.) Parlamentarische Opposition. Hamburg: Hoffmann & Campe.

WIGNY, P. (1972) La troisième révision de la constitution. Brussels: Emile Bruylant.

WINDMULLER, J. P. (1969) Labor Relations in the Netherlands. Ithaca: Cornell Univ. Press.

WOLFINGER, R. (1971) "Non-decisions and the study of local politics." Amer. Pol. Sci. Rev. 65:1063-1080.

ZAPOTOCZKY, K. (1972) "Religion als Grundwert," pp. 162-175 in E. Bodzenta (ed.) Die oesterreichische Gesellschaft. Vienna: Springer Verlag.

ZIEGLER, J. (1976) Une Suisse au-dessus de tout soupçon. Paris: Editions du Seuil.

ZOLBERG, A. R. (1974) "The making of Flemings and Walloons: Belgium: 1830-1914." J. of Interdisciplinary History, 5:179-235.

JEFFREY OBLER is associate professor of political science at the University of North Carolina at Chapel Hill. Dr. Obler earned his Ph.D. at the University of Wisconsin at Madison.

JÜRG STEINER, professor of political science at the University of North Carolina at Chapel Hill, earned a Ph.D. from the University of Berne. Dr. Steiner teaches regularly at the University of Geneva and the University of Zurich.

GUIDO DIERICKX, assistant at the University of Antwerpen, is a Licentiate from the Catholic University of Leuven. He previously served as a research fellow at the University of North Carolina at Chapel Hill.